THE LAST PUNCH
THE LAST PUNCH
THE LAST PUNCH
THE LAST PUNCH

'The Story of Muhammad Ali's
Last and Greatest Fight'

THE LAST PUNCH
THE LAST PUNCH
THE LAST PUNCH
THE LAST PUNCH
THE LAST PUNCH

D0023769

Copyright ©1985 by James Cornelius. All rights reserved, including the right
to reproduction, in whole or part, in whatever form. This work published by the
General Publishing Co., Inc., Atlanta, GA, USA. Published in the USA.

Pictures of Muhammad Ali's last training camp photographed and supplied by
Brenda Foye Cornelius

Notice of Second Publication

Notice is here given that this book, with slight modifications, is being republished
in this form having been earlier copyrighted and published in 1985 by James
Cornelius author, and published by General Publishing Company, Inc., Atlanta,
Georgia USA (2011)

Salute - to my loving wife, Dorothea Salihah Muhammad, who has given of
herself for the past ten years in preparing and improving the book. Her continuing
help and assistance has greatly aided in this publication.

ISBN 978-0-578-09331-4

FORWARD

In 1980 I spent a great deal of time with Muhammad Ali and Minister Abdul Rahman. many of our conversations centered around the passing of the Most Honorable Elijah Muhammad. In 1985 I heard the most compelling speech given by Minister Louis Farrakhan. I always called it "New York '85." Over a period of ten years and my return to the Nation of Islam in 1995 to fully support the work of the Honorable Elijah Muhammad and his servant the Honorable Minister Louis Farrakhan and evolving from hearing the words of the Honorable Minister Louis Farrakhan, his words have led me to believe and to change a significant portion of the Second Edition of the book, Drama in Bahamas, by stating that the Most Honorable Elijah Muhammad is alive.

PREFACE

I first heard of Cassius Clay, who later became Muhammad Ali, while a senior at Atlanta's Henry McNeal Turner High School. June 16, 1964 began like any other day with school, after which I trekked to the Riviera Motel to bus dishes. Many of my high school buddies had fun working there while earning a few dollars to supplement what little income their parents could provide.

I can remember all of the workers perusing the evening newspaper that headlined Cassius Clay's defeat of Sonny Liston, the heavyweight champion of the world. The victory elicited a moment of great pride since most of the waiters were Muslims and thus followers of the Honorable Elijah Muhammad.

A special thanks to my dear friend and personal attorney, the Honorable Bobby Lee Cook, without whose help this book could not have been printed.

Attorney Edward Bob Brooks, a Morehouse College graduate, was at my side day and night to interpret my thoughts over the years of preparation of this material and without his assistance this work would not have been possible.

Dr. Roy Moore of Atlanta's Georgia State University, edited the work, and without his editoral assistance completion of this work would have been extremely difficult.

CHAPTER ONE

DRAMA IN THE BAHAMAS

"ALI PAID ON MONDAY AND 'FIGHT IS ON' " proclaimed the headlines in The Tribune, Nassau and Bahama Islands' leading newspaper on Tuesday, November 24, 1981. According to the Associated Press article, datelined New York:

> "It will take 'an act of God' to stop Muhammad Ali's comeback fight in the Bahamas next month from taking place", according to the head of the company promoting the bout.
>
> Ali was paid Monday as scheduled for his December 11 bout against Trevor Berbick, said James Cornelius, President of Sports Internationale, Ltd., the promoters.
>
> There have been rumors that the fight would not be held. "It's been in a rocky position from day one", Cornelius acknowledged in a telephone interview from Nassau. "But we stood firm, and Ali's standing firmly behind us . . . and at this point in time it would take an act of God if the fight didn't go on."
>
> "Ali got a payment Monday", Cornelius continued. "He has received money in a total of three payments. The rest comes in a letter of credit, which he gets after the fight."
>
> Cornelius would not say how much Ali has received or what his total purse would be. The figure is rumored to be at least $1 million.
>
> The money to stage the fight, Cornelius said, has come from private businessmen and the promoter does not expect to make or lose a

1

great deal.

"We're looking for one thing to give Muhammad Ali a chance to show he just had a bad night when he lost to Larry Holmes on October 2, 1980", Cornelius said. "

Our problems from the very beginning were astronomical. There was a credibility problem."

There has been media opposition to Ali, who will be 40 on January 17, fighting again since the former three-time heavyweight champion did not answer the bell for the 11th round against Holmes.

There have been questions about All's physical condition, but he has checked out to the satisfaction of the Boxing Commission in the Bahamas and has received a license.

Other major problems that needed to be solved were financial arrangements and television coverage.

Television will be subscription, pay cable and limited closed-circuit only, and will be available to 3 million homes in the United States with a gross revenue potential of $10 million-$ 5 million, according to Lionel Schaen, President of SelecTV, in charge of worldwide sales and distribution.

Cornelius said ticket sales are going very well and he expects a sellout at the 17,000-seat Queen Elizabeth Sports Center for the show that also will feature the former World Boxing Association welterweight champion Thomas Hearns and unbeaten heavyweight contender Greg Page."

In May, 1980 Muhammad Ali announced plans to go into the ring again against Mike Weaver the WBA heavyweight champion. Jim Glennie, a California entrepreneur, had called a press conference in New York City for the July 11, date in Brazil. Some money was on deposit and, of course, the "shit was on." After massive media publicity Ali's camp filled with trainers, cooks, masseurs, and cornermen.

The Administration had a problem—the initial deposit by Glennie of Prime

Sports was not acceptable to manager Herbert Muhammad. The problems had begun. Don King soon emerged from Las Vegas with a deal and Prime Sports was out of the game.

Ali's momentum is now broken as the former champion faces a new opponent, WBC heavyweight champion, Larry Holmes. I had gone to the Champ's training camp that summer and found that 38-year-old Ali was in great shape. He could not claim the lightning speed of 10 years ago, but he was in good shape. This ring giant had fought many wars, and knowledge of the ring alone would get him by Weaver, but the uncertainty of the fight interrupted training, bring on a mental strain that is more than the agile body can handle.

Things finally fall into place, on October 2, 1980, at Caesars Palace in Las Vegas.

Ali now sets his sights on a new opponent with a different style that promises a different fight. Herbert Muhammad, Ali's manager for 20 years makes one giant mistake in this important fight—two doctors are needed, but Mr. Muhammad relies on one.

Ali is treated for a thyroid problem, medicine is administered, and the Champ begins to lose weight extremely fast.

On October 2, the morning of the fight, I am in the room with the Champ and Abdul Rahman. It's psyche time.

We discuss what Ali has done for Islam and how Elijah Muhammad fought while among us to establish this religion. Even though these points apparently register with the Champ, I still have a tense feeling in my stomach.

Excitement fills the air in Las Vegas as America's show place fills with her dignitaries, such as Joe Louis (for his last view of the Champ in action), Frank Sinatra, Redd Roxx, Natalie Cole, Wayne Newton, Bobby

Womack, Warren Beatty, and many other actors, singers, oil barons, and oil sheiks.

It's showtime!

Ali's dressing room is filled with cameras and journalists of every shape, size and description. I stood outside and watched the excitement.

It is a scene out of *Rocky* as people—old and young, famous and not-so famous, ugly and beautiful, well-dressed and shabby—clamor to get even a fleeting glimpse of the Champ. The noise, in fact, is almost unbearable, and a claustrophobic would almost certainly die from shock as push becomes shove and melee grows routine. In spite of (or ironically, perhaps, because of) the chaos, the massive crowd seems happy. It has all the aura of war, except no one is suffering or dying, and there are no real enemies. In a real sense, we are all friends with a myriad of reasons for being ensconced in this massive edifice.

Security is tight, but then Las Vegas has always been entranced with security, a status akin to priesthood. In Las Vegas, without security, there is no status.

There is also no status without media attention. Without the bright lights and long-stemmed mikes and screaming reporters, Ali would not be Ali, or at least not the mythical Ali. In fact, it is hard to imagine Ali not facing the cameras and the accompanying electronic equipment and journalists that follow his every move. Interestingly, the media mob appears to form an outer protective shield around Ali with his security personnel and usual entourage comprising a crucial inner circle.

We push toward the front and see a crowd that is the largest ever to witness this type of event. A voice from the back says, "Pick it up Slim!" It's Blood telling me to move faster. The excitement and the crowd momentarily hypnotize me. We move toward the ring as Muhammad slowly takes his last steps toward a face-to-face confrontation with his former sparing partner and now WBC champ.

It will be an event that will mark not only the last confrontation between the two figures, but also the end of an era marred by the worst in man.

It is a moment in history that can be best described as a shooting star that is gone as quickly as it appears but is never forgotten in the minds of the witnesses.

For eleven rounds Ali passively held on as Larry took careful aim, but the Champ rarely returned the punch. The agony was too much for Drew Brown and Angelo Dundee and the towel was thrown in. It was over— Muhammad would never fight again. The press had brought its shovels and was now pouring dirt over their unsung gladiator of many wars.

On that fateful October 3, Ali received visitors as any king or royalty would. I found Howard Cosell desperately trying to see Muhammad, but could not get through. With my assistance in the form of a shout at security, "Let this man through!", Cosell was successful. After the excitement had died, Ali and his bus headed back to Los Angeles.

I deliberately chose to stay around Las Vegas for a few days after the fight. I wanted an opportunity to see this city of glamour, wealth and bright lights firsthand. My stereotyped notions of Las Vegas were strongly confirmed. It is a community that never closes its doors for fear that a chance to squeeze one more dollar out of one more gambler may be missed. Surprisingly, this mini metropolis seemed to have been only lightly touched by the Ali-Holmes fight. Events of this nature are routine in Las Vegas and are accorded little more than the usual two minutes on the local evening news and an in-depth story and accompanying photograph on the front sports page. Big-time gamblers have been known to win as much as $1 million on one bet and just as quickly lose it. Ali was merely another star to arrive in town and depart, once he no longer had any use for the city.

Las Vegas is, above all, a city of lights. It is neon heaven as bountiful signs hawk the wares of the Merchants of Venice. One comes here to dispose of money as though it had been won in a contest that required participants to spend their winnings in the shortest time possible. Las Vegas is a way of life that is enticing and addictive as any pleasure drug. Like a mythical Greek Siren, Las Vegas is charming, alluring and even attractive but just as quickly destroying those who eventually succumb to its singing.

The Ali-Holmes bout was merely another sideshow for the city whose more than 165,000 residents are generally outnumbered by the tourists who flock to its wares at any given time.

Trouble was soon brewing in Atlanta and it was now time for me to ascertain what was going on. Carl Christianson, an FBI agent whom I'd met while testifying in an unrelated bank case, was investigating me. When I called him to see if there were a warrant for my arrest, he answered no, but said I was being investigated and should come immediately to Atlanta. I returned and on October 10, 1980, contacted the United States Department of Justice. I was not arrested but was told the Department was looking into some matters. I was now under great pressure from the Justice Department to tell all I knew about the case they were building against me. I informed the FBI agent and the Federal Assistant District Attorney that all records relating to the loans in question were in storage in California. I began to realize that as long as I could be tracked through my social security number so that if someone checked me through the National Crime Information Center (NCIC) computer, he or she would not find me listed. I approached a friend at the Georgia State Patrol and enlisted his assistance in getting a new driver's license with a new social security number. I was not going to vanish into thin air, but at least I had a chance for a new beginning. I knew I would be a person without a criminal history in Los Angeles. Although my problems were monumental, maybe a new town, a change of scenery, would help. By Christmas Eve 1980, I had packed all my clothes, put my wife and sons in the car and struck out for Los Angeles where we found a nice secluded hotel.

We stayed there for 11 days until we found a house to lease.

My personal problems with drugs mounted but somehow things moved along. We had looked at several houses for rent or lease and finally set our sights on one at 616 South Arden Boulevard, only seconds from where Ali lived. Many days passed, and I eventually went to see the Champ. One morning when I was sitting in his den the Champ looked up and asked me why I had moved to California, but I couldn't tell him the truth—that I was a fugitive from federal and state officials. Instead, I reminded Ali that since he had decided to retire, (I dared not mention that I had heard rumors of his planned comeback), I was ready to begin work on the golf tournament contract he had given me. This struck a bell with him and just as he started to relax, Howard Bing-ham came in excited and out of breath. Howard hurriedly explained that a young Viet Nam veteran was threatening to jump several stories from a Wilshire Boulevard building, just minutes away from Ali's home. Howard had convinced the police that Ali might be able to talk the man down. Ali, Howard and a few other individuals jumped into Howard's car and sped down Wilshire Boulevard to the building. Norman Thrasher (one of the original Midnighters, rock and roll stars of the '50's) and I followed closely behind in my car. Ali jumped from the car and indicated his presence. The Sergeant used his walkie-talkie to get immediate clearance for Ali and company to enter the building to try to talk the young man down. We climbed six or eight flights of stairs and found a frightened young man about to senselessly end his life. I noticed a priest, members of the Los Angeles SWAT team and a group of well-trained crisis specialists. The specialists were trying desperately to coax the young man down. Ali asked and was granted permission to try his hand. He walked to the window which opened onto the ledge where the young man was standing. Ali shouted, "This is Muhammad Ali and ain't nobody gonna hurt you Joe; just let me come out and see you." My heart pounded with fear and apprehension and I watched Ali climb through the window to the ledge. I prayed and wondered if this weak, misguided kid would jump to his death carrying Ali with him. Then I heard Ali say, "I'm coming for you Joe; take my hand, ain't nothing gonna happen to you." Ali gingerly stepped along the ledge and extended his hand. Joe grasped the Champ's hand and followed him into the building. Thank God everyone was safe. I chuckled and thought: "And they say this man, Ali, has brain damage."

I know nothing of whatever happened to Joe. I often wonder, though, if he's still alive or if he eventually managed to take his own life. I do know that he was one damned lucky kid. I firmly believe that Joe had every intention of ending his life then and there. More importantly, he appeared to have the necessary will to carry out his intentions. Even now I am still awed by how Ali was able to quickly and effectively gain the confidence of that young man. I had read stories and seen pictures of people being coaxed not to take their own lives, but even in the movies the task is wrenching and time-consuming.

But for the Champ, plucking Joe back to reality seemed effortless. The irony is that Ali took no credit for saving a life. He approached the task with the same air and confidence with which he faced his opponents in the ring. Ali knew he had to save Joe, even if he risked his own life.

I really wonder if Joe ever realized how fate played a role in preserving his life—how the Champ just happened to be so close by and so willing to go the extra mile to help. I just pray that this kid eventually pulled himself together since God must have truly been watching over him that day.

In January the Champ was called back to Las Vegas for a round in court with the Nevada State Boxing Commission. On another matter, Ray Volpe, the Commissioner of the LPGA, was to meet me in Las Vegas to discuss plans for a golf tournament to be hosted by the Champ. I checked into my room at Caesars and the phone rang. Ray was calling from the Desert Inn to confirm our meeting. The phone rang again. Howard Bingham called to tell me that the Champ was back and ready for our meeting.

The bad news was that the judge ruled for the Nevada State Boxing Commission and Ali would have to surrender his boxing license to the State. Ray and I met for a few minutes to discuss plans for the meeting. We left my room and headed for the Champ's suite. I had hoped for a private meeting, but the usual crowd was there. Thus Ray and I had to discuss our plans openly. After three interruptions, I introduced Mr. Volpe to the Champ. Mr. Volpe, who believed that I had a contract with the Champ, was primarily concerned that the Champ had retired from boxing and would not enter the ring again. Just as I was about to answer his concerns, Harold Smith entered the Champ's suite. He carried a large attaché case in his right hand and documents for the Champ's attorney to look over in his other hand. Harold was preparing to promote a boxing event called "This is it." He opened the case filled with hundred dollar bills and asked the Champ if he needed anything. My eyes bulged with excitement. Harold had tried to get Ali a license to return to the ring. The word was out that Las Vegas had revoked Ali's license. Ten minutes later, after more interruptions, we called it quits. Ray and I decided we were in a madhouse, but with the Champ traveling all the time, we could expect nothing else. The events of the day would not convince me that Ali had given up the sport that made him the most recognized individual in the world and the "retired" athlete who earned the most money in his career.

I think Ray also shared my concern.

We flew back to Los Angeles. I drove my car to Los Angeles Airport and took the Champ back home. Ali seemed concerned about his court appearance, and I wondered about his next step. I was new to Los Angeles and quickly got lost. I eventually pulled over and Ali drove the Mercedes so fast my nerves were shattered when I arrived home.

It was January and little seemed to be happening in my life except that the FBI began to press its investigation. At 6:00 a.m. one day I called the Atlanta FBI office since I was concerned about whether they were going to arrest me. No one would tell me anything, and I really worried. Later that day at Ali's house, the Champ sat staring at the television. "I want to rumble," Ali said.

Ali had gone to Chicago for a hospital visit for what newspapers reported was a minor cold.

The media attention afforded Ali during this time was minimal, in sharp contrast to the continual, intense publicity of the past. Almost any statement, whether newsworthy or not, that the Champ had uttered in the presence of the press until now was almost immediately big news— not just on the sports pages and in the evening sportscasts, but also on the front page and in the regular newscasts. Ali was always big news prior to and during his downfall, and thus I was shocked to see how the Champ was no longer the focus of media attention even when he was admitted to the hospital. When the Champ was at his peak, there was always a barrage of cameras and journalists to follow his every move. Now, however, Ali was worth little more than a minor, back page story or a one sentence item on the local and national news.

I am not privy to how reporters and editors think, but their new attitude toward the "fallen Champ" may have simply been that since Ali would no longer be able to box (thanks to the fact that no one would issue him a license and that no State boxing commissioner would sanction another Ali match), he no longer deserved a forum for his views. The idea that "when you're hot, you're hot but when you're cold, you're out" apparently carries considerable weight with the press.

Whatever the reasons, Ali was cold and out, not only physically but also in the eyes of the agenda-setters and ultimately the public they serve.

Ali needed a fight, and I was determined to help him. I called one of Ali's long time advisors, Jeremiah Shabazz. He felt the best approach was to get an agreement from Ali's manager Herbert Muhammad.

Was I getting into an arena too big for me? Had I watched from the sidelines long enough to carry out this type of event? Was the Prime Sports deal enough experience? Should I stay with the small ventures with which I started?

I called Herbert Muhammad and his blunt reception convinced me I faced a difficult task ahead. I always avoided contacting Mr. Muhammad because I knew he was a shrewd businessman, be we exchanged telexes and we soon reached an agreement.

As the weeks passed, the word quickly spread—Ali was trying to fight again, but who would give him a license?

Ali had offered his services to the big promoters, Don King and Bob Arum, but they turned him down. ABC Sports had also turned him down. Would anyone take another chance with Ali?

I met Donald "Nine" Rolle in Chicago almost a decade ago. His mission at that time was to sell fish, one of his government's great untapped resources, to the Nation of Islam. Donald or "Pro", as I called him, was one of the world's greatest golfers. His distaste for the "PGA" was obvious. He had played with greats like Charlie Sifford and Lee Elder who had broken the racial barriers to the game. Donald and I often discussed a possible fight when I reached him at his "Blue Hill Road" office, the

Southerners Lounge.

I had called "Nine" early for two reasons: he knew Bahamian politics and he personally knew fugitive financier Robert Vesco.

In late April I flew to Nassau. I believed that securing a license for the former Champ would be a breeze. My finances were very limited, and I desperately needed to get the license. After all, I had told the Champ that I could get him licensed. I checked into the Atlantis Hotel, not Nassau's finest, but a moderately priced place that would house me until I finished my business.

There were no room telephones which made privacy difficult, but after all, resort spots are designed for getaways. Unfortunately, after I had been in Nassau for more than a week, the people I needed to contact still seemed elusive. I had been casually introduced by a Los Angeles travel agent to a Mr. Bethel, a hotel manager who was quite familiar with the natives. I had worked with a local attorney who was quite helpful in steering me in the right direction, but as the days went by, I found it increasingly difficult to contact the person in charge of issuing the license.

One day I stopped in the bar of the hotel to play records on the jukebox before going to bed. The manager, Mr. Bethel, introduced me to a friend. I shook hands with a short, chubby gentleman with the air of an African prince. After I had given him a brief rundown on my situation, he indicated he could be of some help with the licensing if I came to his office tomorrow. Earlier I had visited a bar to see my old buddies and long-time friends, "Nine", Bo and Francis. I hailed a cab as one of the locals, Myrt, asked where we were going. Luckily we were going to the same place and Myrt knew the location. I soon arrived in the office of Laventhol-Horwrath, local CPA's, who were talking to Ali in Los Angeles. Mr. Ijeoma, a Biafrican by birth, had been in the Caribbean for many years and was very familiar with the local surroundings. After he made his call, I finally met officials with the Ministry of Youth, Sports, and Community Affairs.

The officials were cordial but business-like in their communication with me. Like all politicians, they were shrewd and tough negotiators. A half dozen or so well-dressed men, who were apparently mid-level personnel who had direct access to the Minister himself. While I never met the Minister, I knew that his assistants would be communicating with him in person or by phone as soon as I had left.

Our discussions resulted in no final agreements, but I felt very optimistic at the end of the meeting, which lasted more than an hour. I knew the license would be granted within a matter of time. I believed I had made some strong, positive and lasting impressions on these individuals that were sure to have a major impact on the decision.

Our conversations began with the usual polite introductions and handshakes, followed by several minutes of small talk regarding my visit. I was careful to make only complimentary comments about the country and my stay, for fear of alienating these governmental administrators. In fact, I had enjoyed the visit, including what little leisure time I had and the marvelous weather and cuisine, but the anticipation and worry were taking their toll. What would it take to get the license for Ali? What did these officials really want? I knew time can often be an enemy, but I was determined to hold fast.

I returned to my hotel for another night of anticipation. The next day I rode the slender elevators to the fourth floor, entered and asked to see Ed Carey. Mr. Carey looked over photographs that I had brought from Los Angeles. I had obtained the photographs for the U.S. Attorney of the Northern District of Georgia and Carl Christianson of the FBI, but I hurriedly scratched out their names and had the Champ to insert new ones for these dignitaries.

During the previous day we had run out of photos. I phoned Ali a second time, and by now the momentum seemed to be building toward this planned "come back". Eventually a bearded individual emerged from his office, and I was given an appointment with the Minister responsible for sports. I would finally be able to make my proposal. I familiarized myself with Centerville, but left early enough that morning to tell my attorney the good news. He was shocked that I had an appointment, although I had been confident all along that a deal could be struck. In the Minister's conference room I was seated at the head of the table with the bearded man seated near the door.

When the door opened everyone stood in apparent relief.

We were now down to business. After a polite introduction and a few bits of small talk with this five-foot titan, I was ready for business.

"I am a nobody from Georgia," I confided. "I have come from Los Angeles to help Muhammad Ali get into the ring again. I have partners in Las Vegas who will be putting the funds together if I can obtain the license." Although I maintained my composure, I was rather awed by the proceedings. I had been under pressure before, including during the earlier preliminary meeting, but the tension was almost unbearable. Although the conference room was somewhat breezy and balmy, I was nervous and hot. I knew that the events that transpired here could have a tremendous impact, not only on my future but on Ali and the boxing world. In fact, this fight had the potential to alter the course of history— the Champ would have one last chance to return!

The conference would compare favorably to a nuclear disarmament meeting in terms of the give-and-take. We all knew that some important matters were at stake, but we wanted to avoid any head-to-head confrontations that would lead nowhere.

More than anything else, I wanted to avoid any real slipups such as promising more than I could deliver or inadvertently insulting someone such as the Minister. I managed to pull myself through by focusing my thoughts on the tremendously positive impact this last hurrah would have not only on Ali but on me. While I did not have visions of sudden fame and wealth, I knew that my career would be on a much more positive track if the deal were exacted and the fight took place as scheduled. The Champ deserved this forum, and I was proud to be a major element in the process. These officials had the means to provide this opportunity, while reaping considerable benefits for themselves and their country.

By the next day I had a signed document that would allow Muhammad All to climb in the ring again, provided certain conditions were met. I was overjoyed, and paid a special visit the next day to Mr. Bethel to offer my sincere thanks and to get him to direct bill my overdue hotel bill.

With the first miracle accomplished, it was time to finalize the plans. John Gardner, the European heavyweight champ, would be an easy foe for Muhammad or any of the top ten heavyweights. Why not match Gardner and Ali and make a fortune?

I had previously met Mingo, an Italian with the compassion of a dove. We had attended the Las Vegas funeral for Joe Louis at the Caesar's Sports Pavilion. Louis 'pallbearers included Muhammad Ali, Frank Sinatra, Sammy Davis, Jr., Larry Holmes and Don King. Jesse Jackson eulogized the "Brown Bomber" as he was affectionately known. I noticed that Muhammad wiped tears from his eyes as the Rev. Jesse Jackson spoke of the battles of "Po-Joe" and how he fought some 54 exhibitions for the Navy and Army relief when black soldiers could be promoted no higher than mere petty officer in these units. Jesse also described how Louis' generous contributions to these causes never brought him any recognition from his country, with the IRS haunting him to his grave. According to the Reverend, "Po-Joe" inspired black children to gather around the radio as he cut his opponents down like the lumberjack of the great north woods cut down trees. "No, 'Po-Joe'—it was you who sent black Americans back to their jobs the next day with pride bursting inside but not the least showing on their faces because of the deep attitude of racial hatred displayed by their bosses," Jackson declared.

As the ceremony closed, Mingo and I openly wept. Many of the participants walked out relieved for America's black hero, but many realizing that the road to civil rights was still rocky. Muhammad appeared angry as he viewed his old sparring partner. I knew then that the Champ really wanted to "rumble".

Most of us were torn between two emotions—sorrow versus relief—as we laid the "Brown Bomber" to rest. Joe Louis was a genuine hero—a man who rose above the intense racial hatred of the times to become in his own way a national model for blacks and whites.

But most of all, Joe was a true black American. Thus we knew we were paying final tribute to a man who in all likelihood would never be matched, in or out of the ring. Yet we all realized that even Joe Louis is mortal, and thus had to meet his Maker in the end.

While it is true that the spirit of a man like Joe Louis lives on, perhaps forever, the fact is that once such a hero has passed away, his impact on those around him and on the profession immediately begins to wane.

None of us will ever forget the "Brown Bomber", but his death marked the beginning of the end of his compassion, his comfort and his inspiration for us all. When Joe died, God surely must have thrown away the mold.

But the sadness was mixed with a sense of relief as well. Joe Louis had suffered mightily, both physically and emotionally, during his last days. His final journey was painful, but his parting brought out the best in all of us. There is no way to fully describe the influence that the "Brown Bomber" had on black America, but, suffice it to say, that when he died, America suffered an incalculable loss.

Back in the Champ's suite the meeting was planned. Thanks to a short chess match to determine who would come from what hotel to start the bargaining for this man's services, Muhammad won—the money would come to him. I left the Riveria Hotel with two businessmen who had expressed an interest in financing this venture. My security man, James, blocked the door to keep out intruders. Since barging in, is commonplace around Muhammad, blocking was crucial.

The meeting started and the big question arose—who would fight Muhammad? Mingo was silent for a moment and then asked, "Where would the fight be?" "Nassau, Bahamas," I replied, "and here are the documents." Then Muhammad chimed in, "ya kno I'm the biggest draw on the face of the earth." Ali said, "they don't wanna see me fight again; whoever, I'll whup him. I'm ready to rumble. "The men thanked us for our time and indicated the talks would continue Monday. Mingo and I left the room smiling with the excitement of schoolboys after their first kiss. I hurriedly changed clothes for the trip back to Los Angeles. On Monday I waited patiently by the phone to learn the details of this new adventure, especially the financial figures. Mingo called that evening and asked to meet with me in Beverly Hills at our regular spot. "Was this it?" I wondered. "Had he gotten the call?" I was optimistic since Mingo had not been anxious to blurt it over the telephone. I had repeatedly warned Mingo not to confirm anything over the telephone. We met for our regular hamburger and coffee at the Hamlet. Mingo had still received no word. "Should I call them tomorrow?" Mingo asked. "Let's give them another day or two," I replied. I did not want to appear to be too anxious. Deep down inside I had the same feeling I had when Ali fought Holmes.

The conversations continued via long distance for two weeks, but our proposition was finally turned down. What would I do now?

CHAPTER TWO

I had talked with Herbert Muhammad earlier that day, and, as always, I remained very positive. I telexed that the funds should be available within 30 days, but I was concerned that I have exclusive right to put this match together. Two days later, after a series of phone calls, the exclusive rights were mine. I employed a Beverly Hills law firm with strong connections in the Bahamas to handle the legal work. The firm had been recommended by an old friend in Houston. Another attorney, whom I had used in the past, suggested a group of investors in Century City for obtaining the necessary collateral. This group would put up the necessary funds . . . I wanted to be protected. After several days of negotiations with the Century City group, my attorney emerged with a deal. We would receive $50,000 each with no percentage of revenues from the fight. I was furious, but with all of my files in his office, I could not determine whether I was being shafted. Later that day I received a call from him and I questioned whether the deal was in our best interest. Suddenly he told me to shut up since he was now running things. My fury calmed to anger, however, as he described his conversation with Charles Lomax, a Chicago attorney who represented Herbert Muhammad. Charles Lomax had apparently given him instructions on how the wheels would turn. The next morning I called Herbert and told him of my fears. I told him how I had flown from Los Angeles to Nassau seeking the license for Ali and how unfair it was for this attorney to move in at the last minute and take credit for all of my labor. My conversation with Herbert, to say the least, was very confusing. After all, this was the same man I had hired to do all of my legal work for the fight, the same man I considered a friend was now on my shit list. For some reason Herbert was sympathetic and sent me a more exclusive contract that specified my rights and clearly put me in the driver's seat. Ironically, I now had an impossible task to perform: the show was now mine and no one would be able to interfere until my time expired. Later that afternoon I spoke with a friend who had been in touch with overseas investors. He had many contracts but was the first to admit that some of these guys had to be screened out. I met with an oriental named Bob. He had visited the house that afternoon and said he had some major bonds for sale that could be used to finance the project.

My optimism and enthusiasm peaked again, and without checking I called Mingo for a meeting to explain the new development. Mingo said he had a friend with a major brokerage house and asked to meet the next day in his offices. Later I spoke with Herbert to reassure him that everything was proceeding well and the funds were at hand.

After two weeks of meeting with Bob and Mingo, though, I reached another dead end. There were no funds. I was determined to find the money somewhere. In my spare time I rehearsed my promotional pitch: "Muhammad Ali is coming back, we are fighting in the Bahamas early October, 1981; the opponent is John Gardner. One helluva show!" But where would I get the money? When I visited an associate's office on Crenshaw Boulevard to borrow gas money I found two reporters from the Los Angeles Times. The major news story was the huge heist from Wells Fargo Bank. MAPS, a company operated by Harold Smith was under investigation for bank fraud. After identifying themselves with calling cards, the reporters asked if I knew Harold Smith and whether Muhammad Ali was broke. Stunned by the questions, I wondered who had lifted the rock from under which these worms had crawled.

I left his office and never returned. Ali had gone to his training camp at Deer Lake, Pennsylvania, to spark some interest in his planned "come back" as well as to inform the press that he would receive a license.

By the weekend, the State of South Carolina had determined Ali's physical condition to be excellent and thus it would allow him to fight there.

When this news hit the newspapers, I wondered what would happen to my project in the Bahamas. I had convinced a local orthodontist that a trip to Nassau was necessary, and he accommodated my needs. In Nassau I stayed in the home of Mr. Ijeoma, a new friend. He and his wife introduced me to a host of executives from all over Nassau on the Yellow Bird, a Caribbean boat that glides up and down the crystal blue-green water on fun-filled evenings. Mr. Ijeoma introduced me as Muhammad Ali's manager. Since this impressed most on board, I was reluctant to cause confusion by clarifying my position. So 1 went along with his kind introduction. Reaction to my plan was mixed but cordial. As we moved to the corner of the vessel, I was introduced to the Vice President of Resorts International. I was unsure whether this huge man was Italian. As it turned out, George Myers was Jamaican by birth but his accent fooled me. When we talked later, we took a short rest near one of the beautiful sandy beaches as many of the passengers took late night swims.

Just as one can be seduced into thinking that a beautiful vacation will last forever, I was awed by the lovely sights, sounds and freewheeling of this paradise. Everyone was obviously thriving on the delectable food and drink, and I must admit I was extremely relaxed. Wouldn't it be nice to be able to eat, drink and be merry in a haven like this while forgetting all of one's toils and tribulations and the world's problems.

While I would occasionally stray back in my thoughts and conversations to my impending project, I spent considerably more time enjoying my conversations with many of the passengers, many of whom I never learned by name. I sensed that this diverse group of individuals shared at least two common traits—all were well-to-do and proud of their wealth.

They all also had an intense love for material things but were nevertheless able to find pleasure in just conversing with one another, viewing the exquisite sunset and just mingling among themselves.

Reality always strikes, and this setting was no exception. By the end of the evening, I began to focus my thoughts on how I could secure the necessary financing for this project. I was glad that I had been able to forget my woes and cares temporarily, but I knew full well that if the deal could not be struck, my future would be bleak. Not only had I invested a horrendous amount of time and effort in this project, but I knew that I was the key to its success— without me, Ali would not get a "comeback".

I dined with Mr. Ijeoma one more evening, while listening to his long stories of homelife in Africa. He also emphasized that his wife was Bahamian, a regular church goer, and an excellent cook. He claimed four lovely children, all with African names and bright futures. I hoped that his initial contacts with me had not been embarrassing for him. In our conversation I stressed that money was being raised on the West Coast, that the stadium facility in Nassau could be improved for a mere $80,000 in U.S. dollars, that Nassau had granted Ali his first chance for a comeback and that we should definitely stage his comeback there!

Many weeks passed before I contacted Mr. Ijeoma. I could have reached him by telephone at his office, but what would I say? Finally, I spoke with his wife at home on a Monday night. As usual, she asked about my family and I inquired about hers. "Please tell Mr. Ijeoma (I breathed a sigh of relief) that things are going well. I will talk with him Wednesday," I commented.

Did I have time for one more week of things are going well? Or was this it? Should I tell him the truth and simply say that Las Vegas had turned Mingo and me down cold, or should I continue to press on all fronts for the funds?

Suddenly, all hell broke loose! ABC announced plans for a Don King promotion: Night of the heavyweights, with John Gardner vs. Michael Doakes. I decided that no more plans would be announced until contracts were signed.

Each morning I left my home about 6:00 a.m. for a five minute drive to Shoney's Restaurant, where I would immediately open my "office" near the restrooms with all the passing traffic. Somehow I survived the squeaky swinging doors and flushing toilets and made the necessary East Coast phone calls. For 24 hours I desperately tried to find funds to promote this event. My pitch to every prospective investor was that funds would be paid back from the live gate revenues or closed circuit television rights. I always stressed that a bundle could be made. By the day's end my telephone bill was sure to enrich Ma Bell since I had called people in ten states. I had already flown to at least that many cities desperately begging for funds. I eventually called my old friend in Houston for names of prospective investors, but he was very cautious in his introductions and very reserved in his approach to any investors.

My prayers were finally answered! I flew to Las Vegas for a Saturday morning meeting with some investors. My lawyers, Ali, and the investors had already held initial conversations. I knew in my bones that the show would go on. I called Nassau and pleaded for one more delay since things were now in place. I landed in Las Vegas around 6:45 a.m. and took a cab to the hotel, walked in the entrance and checked my bags with the bellman. I carried extra clothes in case the meeting lasted more than one day. After all, the conversations had been very positive with Houston. I picked up the house phone and asked for Cameron Adair's room. Cameron and I chatted for a moment and wished one another good luck for a successful meeting.

CHAPTER THREE

We agreed to meet in the Cafe Roma, a restaurant that defies description. Twenty-four hours a day, tall, beautiful women take orders amidst a bevy of gamblers, curiosity-seekers and tourists. Ten months earlier the place had been filled with sports fans and promoters before and after the big battle at Caesars Palace, but now they had been replaced by the usual crowd. There are probably more deals made and broken in this smoke-filled terrain than almost anywhere else in the country except Washington. There is an eerie feeling that immediately descends upon you as you enter this mass of chaos and orderly confusion. There is a blend of the well-to-do among the clientele, and the conversations range from idle banter to high-level negotiations. This place still very much fits the stereotype of the old-time hustling, bustling abode where the great and near-great co-mingle.

I felt basically comfortable in this environment since I knew that any conversations would be private, and the available food and drink made for casual communication. Thus the Cafe Roma was an ideal choice for negotiations of this type. The usual push and shove would not seem so obtrusive, and the meeting was certain to begin on a positive note.

First I was introduced to everyone and then I cautiously proceeded with my well-rehearsed sales pitch for the big event for the Bahamas. My investor, an attractive, tall and angular woman was clearly a shrewd business person, although she could have passed for one of the waitresses in her appearance. She had done her research and surprised me with her questions. As I quickly answered one question and was searching for another, Cameron interrupted as Don King walked in with his distinctive Afro. I told her we would be out of the jurisdiction of the United States Boxing Commission and the big promoters who would swallow this one, lock, stock and barrel.

My answer pleased her since her coaches had already warned her about these poachers.

After King entered, he gave his spiel and iterated that Ali's reign was over. King was apparently unaware of my presence. These harsh words from a man whose very livelihood had once depended upon Ali's battles. King had his word but I had heard enough. Ali would come back. We left the restaurant for an unused conference room, where I could spread my papers from ten different folders. I displayed the documents assuring them I had the rights to this event. She and I shook hands, and 1 agreed to call her Monday for instructions and procedures regarding the financial agreements among ourselves. I had asked for 40% of the profits but would accept 30% as a bottom line figure. Besides the normal $100,000 training expense I would need letters of credit which I felt the Texas group could certainly provide. I flew from Las Vegas to Los Angeles that afternoon, and for the first time, was relieved.

By Sunday afternoon I was discussing Ali's great "comeback" in the Bahamas with Ali himself. We were both so excited that Ali jumped around his den and shadowboxed. "I'll be dancin and weavin—I'm gonna fuck him up," he said. "I'm gonna fuck up the press, the boxing commission, everybody who's kept me from fighting again. We're gonna fuck 'em up!" I left feeling very happy about the whole thing and with my first natural high in a long time. Since Houston is in the Central Time Zone, I could always get a head start with my telephoning. I was in the lawyer's offices early and waiting to get down to business. The telex machine would prove to be invaluable with its quick transmission. We telexed the Houston offices and waited for a reply. In the meeting with the Champ on Sunday, I had told him that funds would be available by Wednesday and that he could look forward to being back in the training camp by the following Monday. I spoke briefly with Mrs. Kerno that afternoon and was told a letter was in the mail. The waiting was killing me! By Wednesday, I still had received no letter. The day of reckoning was at hand and I had no funds. My telephone at home had been disconnected since I had been away all summer. While I was home for a short break, the doorbell rang. My housekeeper answered and was told that Ali wanted me. But what did he want?

I left hurriedly for his house. His gatekeeper knew me now and allowed me in without calling the house. Ali wanted to know what was going on. I assured him everything was fine and that everything would be worked out soon.

For the first time I realized he was losing confidence in me and would soon lose his patience. I went back home with the weight of the world on my shoulders—huge debts, personal problems up to my ears, an FBI indictment hanging over my head, no telephone and no money. During that afternoon I prayed as I had never prayed before, telling the Almighty of my problems, and the good as well as bad deeds I had done.

When I awoke the next day I felt somewhat better. I visited Muhammad and emphasized that I would pull this thing off no matter what if he could have patience.

Unfortunately, my earlier option had run its course and many problems were on the horizon. Herbert had lost patience with me and had told my attorneys there would be no extensions and no more discussions until the money appeared.

Early the next morning I went to Ali's house. Before he had his clothes on, I told him about my charitable contributions in the early days of Islam and how these contributions had brought many problems but strengthened my will. I gently requested that he talk with Herbert about an extension. If so, I assured him I would somehow pull it off.

On Friday I received the long-awaited letter from Houston. Mrs. Kerno offered 10% for my services in return for complete control of the event and an option for the next fight. Although I had spent so much time and effort raising the funds, time was no longer on my side. Thus I had to accede to her demands.

I immediately told my attorneys to accept her offer. There was too little time to look for other investors. Herbert Muhammad asked for $100,000 in cash for Mr. Ali's services. For more than a week he called, wrote, and telexed. There were still no funds. Another false alarm had been set.

I would just have to keep searching.

During the summer of 1980 I made my way around Los Angeles with little trouble. I learned the freeways and eventually could get almost anywhere in the city. My associate from New York, a black burley fellow named Bob Owens, made friends quite easily with his gift of gab. During a trip to Dallas, Bob and I met Richard Chavez, who became a close associate. Richard lived in a gorgeous section of San Bernardino and Bob and I stayed with him that summer so we could plan and execute a golf tournament in Mexico City. Richard was quite familiar with Mexican officials. Our efforts were in vain, but I did see Richard again. Richard, who ran a school in East Los Angeles, was always willing to help. So I had approached him with the idea of the fight in Nassau.

Many of my financial problems hung in the balance with that Tuesday meeting with Richard. When I left Richard's office to go back home that afternoon, I had no gas, no money and very little food. I had asked Richard for a $15,000 loan to carry me through until financing materialized for the fight. I prayed all the way to Richard's office. When I arrived, I was told that Richard's partner had left $5,000 for me, and Richard would get the rest from his bank. My wife, who had always been my strongest supporter and third eye, followed me in our rented Pinto as Richard and I drove to the bank. When we received the money, my wife cut the engine off. When I told her that we might be able to go back for cheaper gas, she looked at me in disgust and coasted into the Shell Station adjacent to the bank. We weaved through the freeway traffic as tears rolled down her face—the day had been trying. However, I knew that this was only the beginning of an up-hill battle. When we returned home, I paid my old attorney in full. What a pleasure! We immediately had the telephone connected, shopped at Ralph's Supermarket, and conducted the usual business.

I made many attempts that week to find funds for the fight. My new attorneys had made some calls, but nobody was interested.

I met with Jay Foonberg who passed on verbatim statements from some of Ali's "close" advisors regarding Ali's health and who would and would not make money from Ali in the future.

Was I barking up the wrong tree? Had I bitten off more than I could chew?

Norman Thrasher, an old friend from Atlanta, was now living in Detroit. A singer in the rock 'n roll days of Little Richard, The Flamingo's, and Chuck Willis, Thrasher was a great balladeer. He was also always willing to give me advice. When I called Norman from my office at Shoney's, he was always optimistic and inspiring. "Keep your prayers up, James," he said. "Keep reading (the Holy Quran), keep on pushing, you'll make it."

With the prospects of funding now apparently out of reach, I became desperate. I visited Ali's and told him everything had been arranged. I had to deceive him into thinking that the deal had been finalized.

"Champ, will you fight Trevor Berbick?" I asked. "He's the guy that just took Larry Holmes 15 rounds in Las Vegas." I realized that since the John Gardner fight had been stolen from under us, if Ali could fight a man as strong as Berbick, the press criticism would die down. No one considered Berbick a bum.

Without any hesitation, Ali said yes. But by the next day I detected some hesitation in Ali's voice regarding his new opponent. I talked with

Herbert that same morning. According to him, "Berbick is too tough. Besides, I haven't seen a dime yet, and you don't know anything about the boxing game anyway."

I was very upset when I left the house since I had worked all summer to help him get started again. No one had been willing to help him but me, and now he was criticizing me. When I reached home, I immediately called Herbert. "What's this about Berbick?" I inquired. His answer was very logical. "Ali's long layoff after the Holmes fight, Berbick's tough stand against Holmes, and the close decision in Las Vegas in favor of Larry Holmes are just too much for the Champ to take on right now."

I reluctantly agreed for the time being. If Ali had any fighting ability left, I would certainly not squander it on a nobody. He could get hurt as easily with an unranked boxer as he could with Trevor Berbick.

My mind was now made up. If it were God's will that the fight took place, Muhammad Ali would go out as a credit to the sport and not be embarrassed later in the history books as a man who sought a few million dollars for fighting a softy.

I left the next day to establish a new office. My telephone at home had been disconnected again and Shoney's was just not private enough.

Earlier in the year I had bummed around Los Angeles with Kevin Jackson. He lived in Hollywood, and we could always depend on one another for small favors.

I set up shop in his home, which was only ten minutes from my house. I soon learned that John G. LaBreque was Trevor Berbick's manager. I understood that Mr. LaBreque was a promoter and used car salesman—a jack of all trades. I tried to reach him by telephone for two weeks since I knew the standard operating procedure is to talk to the manager first. When I finally reached him, his voice was faint, and in spite of his accent, I understood him. His voice rose considerably when I mentioned

Muhammad Ali. Mr. LaBreque said he represented Mr. Berbick and would be seeing him in Halifax next week. I explained to this French-speaking Canadian that his heavyweight champion had to be signed very quickly because of time constraints. I received telegrams the next day of those assurances. I also made a $25,000 guarantee to Mr. LaBreque for the delivery of his fighter at the planned press conference at the Waldorf Astoria on September 1, 1981.

By charging telegrams to Kevin's telephone, I made reservations for a conference room at the Waldorf, and after some finagling had reserved rooms for everyone flying from Los Angeles to New York for this big event. During the next few days I rode around Los Angeles ordering stationery, getting press folders printed and making all the necessary arrangements for the New York press conference.

This press conference was crucial since it would make it or break it for me. As far as I was concerned, no detail was too small to be overlooked. I spent day and night on the arrangements and contacted literally hundreds of people, including every member of the press I could think of. All eyes would be focused on this event, and I was at the center of the storm.

I survived on as little food and sleep as possible, while realizing that all of this pressure would eventually take its toll. But I had no choice. This press conference had to tick like a new clock or all my fortunes (at least as I had envisioned them) would be down the drain.

I may have engaged in overkill in my preparation, but I would make damn sure that when the cameras rolled and the spotlight focused on Ali and Berbick, there were absolutely no hitches. Even the color and quality of the press folders became an obsession—after all; the medium is sometimes the message. I made call after call to the Waldorf's personnel, and even though I knew I was making a pest of myself, I had to be assured that all the necessary arrangements had been made and the requisite facilities and equipment available.

I have learned that one of the most effective ways of mollifying a critical press, especially in the sports world, is to provide them with a slick production that can evoke little criticism. We all like to be entertained, and the press nearly always responds positively to a good show, even if controversial. My friend Kevin agreed to walk into the press conference as if he were my bodyguard. His muscular 5'6" frame fit the stereotype. Our routine was well rehearsed. The momentum was now building, and some of my earlier contacts were paying off, not with funds, but with a great deal of interest and energy.

For example, Paul Dothseth at Third World Investments on Stocker Street, a West Los Angeles district that houses many black businesses had struck up a good friendship. Paul had contacts all over the world and could maneuver as well as I could when things had to be done. We met in Culver City one afternoon where I secretly disclosed plans for the Nassau fight. He expressed confidence in my ability to achieve my plans and immediately rolled up his sleeves to help. First and most importantly, he tracked down cable and closed-circuit operators. Paul was magnificent on a pay phone, and my Shoney's office looked like child's play compared to his Tiny Nalors. For several days, we were regular customers of family restaurants all over Los Angeles. Our first meeting which included cable and closed-circuit television rights and just plain ol'cash on the agendas took place five blocks from my house at the home of Richard Marks, a long-time friend of Paul's. As with most Los Angeles business deals, one guy knows another guy who knows another. I was irritated that I had to explain this relatively simple venture to someone and again to a room filled with individuals who "knew someone". Fortunately, Paul was very familiar with the situation and his introduction was impressive. Then I made my pitch. Everyone was silent as I enunciated about the great "comeback". People were now interested! I left the meeting with a renewed spirit. Paul and I agreed to celebrate at Chason's, a well-known restaurant in Beverly Hills. With my spirits high and my confidence renewed, I was ready to end the night with flair. I was very excited until we pulled in front of Chason's and found that President Reagan would be dining there that evening. My heart fluttered as I passed L.A.'s finest all lined up to guard the President. I had never seen so many police officials in my life. Paul and I waited for friends to join us at the bar and we both had a drink. I tried to calm my nerves by convincing myself that after all, only the FBI and other state agencies were looking for me. But I was haunted by imaginary headlines, "PRESIDENT'S DINNER INTERRUPTED BY ARREST OF MAN WANTED BY FBI."

How could I enjoy my dinner? As the evening progressed, I moved close to the bar, where secret service agents were stationed. I soon relaxed, and Paul and I reflected on a very exciting day.

Eventually we moved up from eating at Tiny Nalors and the family joints to Scandia, a West Hollywood hot spot. Paul had talked about this place as if it were the Taj Mahal, and I could hardly wait. I was introduced one evening to John Ettlinger and many of the regulars at this haven on Sunset Boulevard. Ettlinger was the President of Medallion TV, and I pondered how he could get so much done all day on a bar stool. Richard (Marks) asked me if I had the bout agreement.

"If you have it," he noted, "I can raise all the money in the world." Richard had dealt with the owners of the Olympic Auditorium in Los Angeles, who were premier boxing promoters. After I had made my usual sales promotion and progressed to investment schemes, I was at a loss to go further since I had no real financial backing.

I had no choice but to secure Muhammad's signature. Even though he had told people he would fight again, I had to have an agreement in writing before I could get the funds I so desperately needed from the cable company or the banks. Richard had struck a responsive chord. "Raise the $100,000, give it to Ali and maybe the financing for the venture will fall into place," he continued.

I returned home on Monday afternoon and once again desperately tried to raise the $100,000 by telephone. I called several cities in an effort to nail down a one-month loan, but I had no luck. It would have been easier to jump over the moon.

By Wednesday night I was still telephoning for money at home. Finally, the telephone rang. Cyril from Nassau had not heard from me and was furious. He insisted that the Minister wanted to see me and that the Minister would fly from Freeport for a meeting with me on Thursday morning in Nassau. "If I didn't make the meeting,"he warned, "I had better never come to Nassau again." I slammed the phone in disbelief. How could I get to Nassau with no money?

CHAPTER FOUR

The travel agency had refused to give me credit; there was no money in the house and no one from whom to borrow money. When I called the airline, I discovered the ticket price was $742.00 round-trip Los Angeles to Nassau, and because of customs regulations, I was required to purchase a round-trip ticket. With $44.00 in my pocket, 1 was $698.00 short.

It was now 9:30 p.m. and the Pan Am flight left Los Angeles for Miami at 11:00 p.m. with a change of planes in Miami Thursday morning and arrival in Nassau at 9:30 a.m. I phoned a couple of friends, but they were broke as well.

Once again, the clock was ready to strike, and I was in a defenseless position. Money always seemed to elude me, but I had been able to make some last minute maneuvers in the past that had redeemed me.

All I could hope for now was a miracle. I had no liquid funds and no assets to secure ready cash, and none of my friends were in either the requisite financial condition. Or the frame of mind to provide me with the fare.

Since all of my efforts had failed and the deadline was drawing near, I decided I had no alternative but to drive to the airport and hope for a viable idea to strike me. Before I left home, I gave my wife $34.00 since I knew she needed some money just to survive while I was gone. I kept $10.00 since experience had taught me that no one should ever travel broke. Even a phone call costs money, and how do you live without food?

By the time I arrived at the airport, lightning had struck. I would write a check and hope that the airline would not check my bank to ascertain my credit worthiness (or lack of it).

I had left early (around 9:45 p.m.) for the airport, and thus I had sufficient time to execute my plan without arousing suspicion. Even though the check would quickly bounce, I would already be in Nassau and could certainly manage there.

My thoughts now focused on the tearful departure I had made from my wife that evening. She insisted that I keep all of the money since "there is food in the house." I assured her that I would call home the next day. Hopefully, the telephone would be connected for at least another week. After I tipped the skycap $2.00, 1 waited in a long line to purchase a ticket. The airline agent appeared hostile looking and this frightened me. I left the line to call my travel agent. "Please prepay a ticket for me," I asked in a soft voice. "James, I just can't go any further" she replied. I was determined to find another way. I re-entered the line, realizing that if I did not convince the agent to take my check, I was finished.

It was 10:35 p.m., and my plane was scheduled to leave at ll : 04 p.m. The line was moving slowly and time was running out. As I approached the counter, a new face appeared. As I stepped up to the counter, I began to explain my situation. I told the agent that I had recently moved to Los Angeles and had an out of state license and needed to write a check. He asked my destination. "Nassau, Bahamas, sir," I quipped.

"That fare is $742.00 round trip," he replied, "and we only accept checks with a major credit card up to five hundred dollars for ticket purchases. I'm sorry!"

My life flashed before my eyes. This was it!

I looked at him directly in the eyes and began to tell him that I had recently moved from Georgia. Just as I was about to say my credit card had been lost, he stopped me. I had struck a responsive chord. "You're from Georgia?" he inquired. "Yes, I was born there and I went to college there." We soon discovered that we had gone to the same school. We didn't know each other, but it made no difference. I had an opportunity to elaborate on my predicament. "I am promoting a fight in Nassau, I noted, "and it is imperative that I get on that 11:04 flight to Miami. I have a Georgia driver's license with no photo on it and my check is on a California bank." I opened my briefcase and displayed the letter that Mr. Nottage had provided in April, although, it was now late August it made no difference. I put everything in front of him. He looked at me and said for some reason, "I'm going to take a chance on you. "Please make sure this check is good, or it will cost me my job." I thanked him at least three times and silently thanked God Almighty.

By 10:55 p.m. I had a ticket, but the flight left in nine minutes. As I dashed through the corridor, I was crying. I had no money and my option with Herbert would expire on Friday. I resolved to keep searching until then. I boarded the plane literally before its departure and flew into Nassau the next morning on Bahamas air.

Mr. Ijeoma waited patiently for me outside the Nassau Airport in his vintage Mercedes.

"How are you, my brother?" he asked. "I am fine Cyril. Things are going well," I replied. With $8.00 in my pocket I knew I was lying. We drove off and I felt great as I breathed the beautiful Nassau air and heard the ocean roar. Mr. Ijeoma informed me of the Minister's concern that he had not heard from me. He said I must see him and explain what was going on. Until now, I had met with the Minister only in the presence of his cabinet and staff. I had never faced him one on one.

I rehearsed my speech over and over again. Before I left Nassau with the documents in early May, the Minister had warned me not to ask for any funds for the fight promotion.

Now I had to tell him that in spite of all my travels, the money was unavailable elsewhere. We pulled up to Centerville, House; I told Cyril absolutely nothing of my plans as we rode all the way from the airport. As Cyril and I sat down I wondered if my journey was at an end. After all, the Minister had been very firm in his insistence that his government not be approached for funds! When the Minister entered the room, Cyril and I stood and then we all sat down together. "How are you Mr. Nottage?" I inquired. "Not so good!" he shouted. "I have heard nothing from you since you left for Las Vegas to get the funds to promote this fight. Well!"

"Ah, Mr. Minister, Sir, I've been everywhere trying to raise the money and if I could get $100,000 I could make this thing happen," I remarked.

"Are you asking me for the funds?"

"Well 'er Sir, I mean I'm asking the Bahamian Government to put it up.'

I had finally blurted it out with the courage of a Bengal tiger. "Ha! Ha! Ha! That would take going to the general treasury, exchange control approval, all kinds of Government approval, that's impossible!"

"Well, Mr. Minister, it's like this. If I could raise $100,000 for Ali's contract I could then go to a cable TV company and get the funds needed to promote this thing properly."

The Minister was interrupted for an overseas call, and Mr. Ijeoma followed him.

One of the most irritating aspects of this albatross around my neck had been the constant interruptions when I was communicating with various honchos, whether on the phone or in person.

Here was another one, but it had one positive side effect: it gave me the opportunity to collect my thoughts and attempt to develop a new strategy. Quite frankly, I was stumped. I had given my best shot, only to be interrupted and held in agonizing suspense.

Was the call related to the project or was it regarding another matter? Surely, the Minister would not have chosen to leave unless the call had been either extremely important or tied in directly with the matter at hand.

I have never been an extremely patient individual, but this project, which had certainly taken its toll of my psyche and my personal life, had conditioned me to calm down, bite my tongue and hold on tight when the suspense tried to overwhelm me. Nevertheless, seconds seemed like minutes and minutes felt like hours as I remained en-scounced in my chair.

I had thoroughly convinced myself that I could do little at this point than allow fate to ride its course. I had done my best, short of selling my soul to the devil, and that is all that anyone can do.

Finally they both re-entered the room. The Minister looked me directly in the eyes, said he believed in me and knew I could pull it off.

"I have asked Mr. Ijeoma to find some local Bahamians to put up the funds," he said.

It had happened! Thank God for a second miracle! It was now late Thursday, and my agreement with Herbert ran out on Friday. I would have to work fast.

Mr. Ijeoma provided me with lodging for the night. Tomorrow the action begins—promoting, contracting, laughing, crying—the whole works!

Early the next morning I met with my new partners. Frankie Wilson was senior managing partner of the firm of Laventhol, Horwrath, Haskins and Sells, of which Mr. Ijeoma was a member.

Mr. Wilson, an astute Bahamian businessman, had convinced a New York associate to be a shareholder. Mr. Ijeoma brought aboard Charles Major, Jr. and Charles Major, Sr., local promoters with fifty years' experience in the business.

Our team was set, and our first business was to call Herbert Muhammad and Michael Phenner.

Now I could be proud that $100,000 was in the bank and we could meet in New York to hammer out a contract. I was now President of Sports International Bahamas, Ltd., a name that I had conceived while in Los Angeles.

What a joy! What hope! Ali can return to the ring. Several meetings were convened during the day. As the talks continued I began to feel uneasy about Mr. Wilson.

If I had been made President of the company, why was Mike Phenner told that Wilson was boss. After all, we had agreed to make our decisions mutual. At 5:00 p.m. Friday Mr. Ijeoma and Mr. Wilson were reassured that if the funds were provided to Muhammad Ali, cable companies would finance the venture.

It was only 2:00 p.m. in California and I had Paul waiting with Richard Marks to confirm that a deal could be made if we had Muhammad Ali's signature. Paul had worked very closely with John Ettlinger and although I didn't have the final word I sensed it would come.

After a few more calls and meetings I left Nassau for Los Angeles on the 8:15 p.m. flight to make final arrangements for the press conference and the trip to New York.

My wife and family were waiting at LAX to pick me up. Everyone was excited!

I had woken early Sunday morning to read the stories about the Hearns-Leonard fight. I had watched the fight at a friend's house the night before and left as excited as the fans who viewed it live in Vegas.

The morning passed quickly and then someone knocked at the door. My telephones were disconnected, and if anyone wanted to see me, he had to come to the house. Howard Bingham had come by to warn me of a meeting at Muhammad's house at which Don King and Charles Lomax "would try to set me up." Howard had very little time to explain, but emphasized that I must be careful.

I know that fate can take strange twists and turns at times, but this bit of discomforting news was the straw that broke the camel's back.

I had expended an extraordinary amount of time, energy and even money to finally be within touching distance of my goal and now an outsider was attempting to screw me! What unmitigated gall! I was so upset that I considered all kinds of options from chucking the whole deal to personally lambasting Mr. King. But by this point, no force short of God Almighty was going to stop me from my appointed rounds.

I had come too far and had too much to lose to allow any obstacles, whether major or minor, to impede me.

In times like this, I have always been able to muster my strength and endure. I immediately snapped my mind into the command mode and replaced any fear and doom I may have had with renewed spirit and optimism.

I was no newcomer to this game, but rather a seasoned veteran who had learned from his mistakes.

I had heard Mr. King the week before on a CBS sports show with Jim Hill. According to Mr. King, Muhammad Ali was a great citizen of the world whom he admired, but he would never get involved in a promotion involving Ali.

I ran upstairs to get dressed, but before I could get my shirt buttoned, the doorbell rang again. My mind was reeling.

"Howard was right, they are trying to set me up," I mumbled. I could hear Drew Brown in the foyer telling my wife that Don King was waiting for me. Drew claimed everyone was concerned only that Ali's opponent, Trevor Berbick, was too strong for Ali.

Before Drew could mutter his next sentence, I jumped down two flights of stairs to reach him and had him collared. I was ready to kick his ass, but my wife managed to separate us.

I threw on my sport coat and left for Ali's. When I got there, Ali's Rolls Royce was being parked. I walked down the steps with Ali and reminded him I had told him the venture would succeed. We were soon in a car headed for LAX. I chose to ride in the back seat. The Champ rode with King in front. Mr. Lomax sat behind Ali.

"Cornelius, I want you to meet Mr. Don King," Ali said. I softly said, "hello, pleased to meet you sir." (in my Southern drawl)

"Cornelius, what we want to do is change the opponent," King said. "I understand that you have no boxing arena in Nassau, only a baseball field. I want to help you!"

I was furious as I thought of all my hard hours of work.

Mr. King went on to say that Trevor Berbick was too tough for Ali and that he had an opponent for Ali named Bernado Marcado. "Ya see I got him rated number 10. He will be easy for the Champ to hit," King claimed.

When he closed his mouth, I began to talk. My anger was apparent as I directed my conversation to Ali.

"Champ," I emphasized, "this is the same mother fucker who was on CBS last week talking about you being finished in boxing and now he's trying to muscle his slimy way into the fight! And he brings this rotten ass Lomax with him."

I could see Lomax out of the corner of my eye, squirming as I talked. "I'm not changing a damn thing!" I shouted.

Don became very cool, telling Ali that I was playing him for a chump! "A chump!" I shouted.

"Mother fuck you, you black son of a bitch."

"Mother fuck you," he shouted back.

By now Ali had entered the conversation and asked for calm. He diplomatically asked me if I knew to whom I was talking.

I was vehement.

"Yes!" I shouted.

Ali and I went back and forth for a couple of minutes and we eventually pulled into the airport.

As Mr. King left the car, he extended his hand for a shake.

I reluctantly shook, and we said goodbye since his plane for Cleveland was on schedule, there would be no time for me to walk to the concourse with him.

What a relief!

Ali waited as I climbed into the front seat.

As we pulled away, I began to break down and tears began to stream down my face as I reflected over the day's trials and tribulations.

Ali asked, "Who are you to tell me what to do? Don't you know who I am? I get rid of niggers like you all the time. Do ya know what you're messing with?"

I desperately tried to hold the tears back, but I could not stop sobbing. "Champ, you're right," I cried. "I am a nobody, but I told you early this summer that when all of this happened and after I went through the trouble of putting this together, they would try to take it away."

"I expressed my faith and hope in life in people like you, people who didn't take the easy way out. Sportswriters would laugh us clear out of the ring with any other opponent—but Champ I've always said you're the boss. I put it all together, but you can have it."

In my mind and heart I had been to the mountain top.

We rode a few blocks and were nearing his Hancock Park mansion when he looked in the mirror and said, "Hey, I think I can beat Berbick."

I was speechless as we pulled into his driveway. I dashed home to tell my wife of the day's developments.

On Sunday night LAX was madhouse with hundreds of friends, well-wishers and aides ready to board the flight to New York for the fireworks! I arrived in New York relieved my battle scars had not been permanent. I was to meet Ali and Howard Bingham, a skeptic from the first day. Howard was a good guy at heart. He had been with Ali some 17 years and was really concerned about Ali's welfare. Ali and I were always saying, "We're gonna fuck 'em up." Howard was our strongest critic.

"They are going to fuck you up," Howard would always respond. Later that day we would be meeting "to fuck Howard up".

(Round One) We made arrangements all weekend to get the contracts finalized in time for the big announcement. The Waldorf Astoria would be our meeting ground. All weekend we hammered out Ali's contract under the supervision of my Los Angeles and New York attorneys and Ali's Chicago attorney. By working around the clock we had reached an agreement around 2:30 p.m. The big moment was now at hand. I informed Mr. Phenner that once the press conference was over, I would resign as President of Sports Internationale Bahamas, Ltd. I knew that if my name were ever published, the FBI might disrupt the promotion. I would simply remain in the background until everything was over. The press conference began.

CHAPTER FIVE

MUHAMMAD ALI'S PRESS CONFERENCE ON
SEPTEMBER 1, 1981 AT THE NEW YORK WALDORF

PHILLIP DAVIS: "Ladies and gentlemen of the press corps of the United States and elsewhere, I would first wish to thank you for patience in awaiting our arrival to this press conference, and I would like to thank you all for coming here today on such short notice. My name is Phillip Davis, and I am the general counsel for Sports Internationale Bahamas, Ltd., and we have an exciting announcement to make this afternoon. Sports Internationale Bahamas, Ltd. is happy and gratified to inform you and the world that the Government of the Bahamas saw fit to grant permission to Muhammad Ali to stage his first fight on the comeback trail to regain once again the World Championship.

The bout is to take place in the Commonwealth of the Bahamas. Sports Internationale Bahamas, Ltd. is also gratified and deeply indebted to the Government of the Bahamas for having extended this permission to have Muhammad Ali to fight in the Bahamas, and indeed our thankfulness and gratitude is magnified by the fact that they were unable that he Muhammad Ali . . . was unable to obtain such permission in the United States before the Bahamas granted it to him. I would like on behalf of Sports Internationale Bahamas, Ltd. to extend my thanks to Muhammad Ali for launching his, the greatest comeback in the history of boxing, in the Bahamas.

Sports Internationale Bahamas, Ltd. would therefore like to thank the Government of the Bahamas and, in particular, the Minister of Youth, Sports and Community Affairs, the Honorable Senator Kendall W. Nottage for their support in this endeavor. The Honorable Senator Kendall Nottage would like very much to have been here today. However, he regrets that prior commitments prevent his attendance. In recognizing Mr. Ali's continued contribution to and support of youth programs around the world, Sports Internationale is proud to be associated with a man of Mr. Ali's stature, who has always been a friend of the Bahamas.

We feel that this world class event will reaffirm that the Bahamas is one of the sports and vacation capitals of the world. We are presently in negotiation with several of the world's top heavyweight contenders, some of whom have already verbally confirmed the willingness to have Mr. Ali as an opponent. Muhammad Ali has expressed his desire to commence his training for this fight in the Bahamas shortly after his return from Hong Kong, which he intends to travel to in the very near future. Ladies and gentlemen, this is a historic moment for the Bahamas and, having spoken to Mr. Muhammad Ali, a historic moment in his life in his once again comeback trail towards the championship of the world. Muhammad Ali is well known to all of you; so he needs very little introduction—ladies and gentlemen, kindly welcome with me to the lectern—Mr. Muhammad Ali.

MUHAMMAD ALI: Thank you. First of all, I want the people, members of Sports, Mr. Nottage of the Bahamas for granting me a license to pursue my aspirations and dreams. Also I want to thank first the Government of Columbia, South Carolina. Also and, ah, the people involved there who granted me a license also.

First of all, you probably know—as always I've shocked the world ever since the Sonny Listen fight and some twenty-one years later I continue to stun the world. I love challenges—don't give me a challenge—don't tell me I can't do nothing—don't tell me it can't be done— then I'm out to prove you're wrong and I'm right it can be done. So I've made my first victory. Now, I heard a thing once—if you get a victory and ah, ah, opportunity over your adversary, then in thankfulness to God for, forgive 'em—so I forgive you. (LAUGHTER) Now, I would like to open this little time up for questions and answers because I know there are many and I, ah, wrote a little speech that I wanted to give concerning WHY. Everybody's question is why—Champ, why? Why? Because it's there—Why? Because no man will probably never see another chance—Why do we go to the moon—because it's there! Now, why are we not satisfied? They say Champ, three, ain't three enough? Well, ain't the moon enough? Why Mars? Because it's there. Why Saturn, Venus? Because it's there. Why am I going four times— because no man has ever been great enough to do it four times—no man. It's something I gotta do! When I'm an old man like most of you all ssssssitting back saying—man I shoulda took a shot! Because another person says something is wrong with you don't mean its right. The real basis is what are you thinkin*? Too many children today got big problems in this country, drop out of school; because work is hard they drop out of studies. I wanta be inspirational. I've always tried to be inspirational to people. When I challenged the Vietnam war it looked bad—it turned out to be right—help a lot of—many white boys, namely come to me—Champ, I'd a ran to Canada like the rest of'em but I saw you fight this thing out. I fought it too—they stood up. When I first fought Sonny Listen I was gonna be killed. It couldn't be done. Sonny Listen knocked out Floyd Patterson twice—Zoro Foley knocked his— trouble beat up policemen—one fist bigger 'en both of mine—man he'll kill that kid Cassius Clay. What did I tell ya—I'm the greatest. I'm pretty. You said I was crazy, didn't you? Liston thought I was crazy too. He wouldn't get off the stool in the eighth round—seventh round. Then here comes the draft fight. Three and a half years off—came back with Frazier got knocked down—got beat the last night—now I'm really finished. Three and a half years off with Frazier—three and a half years off, knocked down by Frazier—he's through—then Norton broke my jaw after Frazier—now you know I'm through—Norton beat him—I said I'm not through—I wouldn't let you tell me I'm through—too many people tell

45

their children you'll never be nothing— you've been told by your mother and father you'll never be nothing, and that impression remains and they don't be nothing—don't tell me I can't come back and beat Norton two more times—beat Frazier two more times—then George Foreman—Oh he's too old, too much pounding, three and a half year layoff, two Frazier fights, two Norton fights—Foreman'll kill him—he knocked out Frazier twice—what'd I do—beat Foreman.

Okay, then came Spinks. Now you know I'm finished—wut'n dancin at all, did the rope-a-dope—that's his excuse his legs are gone. I said it's not, I'm not finished. I came back and danced fifteen rounds at thirty-six years old with Spinks. So don't be surprised as why I'm here. I never been a quitter. I've always liked challenges. I'm of being courageous, of being daring, of being bold. This is bebebefitting that I take such a challenge, so I'm so happy when the people say—I see cartoons in the paper—Gallo—old man long beard. Do I look like an old man to you? With a long beard whole lot of gray hair? Got a couple little grays but basically I'm still in, still in, still nice looking man. I with that. .. and let me tell you somethin else—they say, Champ, I say why not? Why you so so against me fightin. You looked so bad in your last fight— I looked so bad! What if I put my arms up and said I quit and walked out—Mannnn—what if I just said I quit—could I be fightin a couple more months later? No—so—what if I got knocked down and crawled around the ring—I ain't gon name no names—you know even in the Holmes fight that bad night I didn't get hurt—I didn't get hurt. Had a little bruise and wudn't fightin—sick and didn't—tell you somethin else nobody wrote—went eleven rounds and didn't sweat—I'm sweatin now—see me wipe my face—I'm sweatin now more than I did the night I fought Holmes—A—ha ha ha—AA—I swear—I didn't sweat this much. A 114 degrees heat—eleven rounds and dry! I was ter—some-thin was terribly wrong with me. I couldn't move—I couldn't fight— I couldn't fight—I couldn't, couldn't—now if that was the best I could do you right, I should never get in the ring again—if that was my b— man I got—I'm weighing 240 pounds now, and 1 can do better at this moment than did that night—I didn't even jab. I didn't even tho jabs— I didn't do nothing. Okay—so they say I had a bad night, so don't fight no more? I'm prove 'em wrong—now—

REPORTER: Someone had called for an opponent?

MUHAMMAD ALI: Well, we'd hate to call names cause it makes 'em great—when I call a name it makes you big—they become famous—they get in all the papers—they read about it in Russia and China—they start saying' I want 12 million. Do you know until I started wudn't no ten million dollar talk—five million dollar talk? When I fought Frazier the first time, me, and Herbert Muhammad fought for two and a half million—was big news—now everybody—little welterweights say I want ten million.

REPORTER: Muhammad, is it that you just want to come back one more fight to prove and show the public that you can really—still fight?

ALI: No, I don't have to prove that—I've been made so popular by Allah, God—I'm so great with people—they don't want me to—I don't need none. I can go out there now—I challenge any celebrity, white or black, to follow me—let's take a walk anywhere in the world and see who stops the traffic—I mean, I don't need that—It's the four-time title—do you know what's gonna happen when they say ladies and gentlemen? Ding, ding, ding, ding—ladies and gen—the crowd hollers hrrrrr—ding, ding—hrrr - hrrr - ding, ding, ding—nn miracle four-time World champ Muhammad All!—hrrrrr—do you know I'd be the biggest athlete in the history of the recorded records of the world? This is somethin' I gotta take—I gotta take a shot at it. I can't give this up—do you know, do you know that boxing went one hundred years before man won it twice? I—you know I stopped the saying in boxing—one minute—they never return—

remember that thing in boxin—they never return—didn't—I stopped that—they can't say that no more—I the only man that stopped that sayin—they never return— I changed the whole world—okay—now do you four-time Champion tha's why—it's not that I miss the crowd or I need the money or I—I need or want the roar—naw—it's the four time title to have that record in—mmm—the Boxin' Hall of Fame—four time Boxin' Heavyweight Champion—Man, that's all I see, and I know I can do it—cause Holmes is getting old! (LAUGHTER)

REPORTER: Ali, when do you plan on fighting? There's no day, no month, no year even announced—when are you coming back?

ALI: What did—what did we decide on fellas?

CYRIL IJEOMA: December 2.

ALI: We have a fella that—I picked the toughest guy I could find that Holmes couldn't knock out—I said I knock him out and come back. That's a good way to come back—guy named Trevor Berbick bad strong guy, black guy from Canada—where is he from?

DAVIS: Halifax.

ALI: Yea, took Holmes fifteen hard rounds and had him going, and I picked a tough one befittin of a Champion—I didn't look for no softy—give me the baddest one you can find other than Holmes— Trevor Berbick—that's who—what'd you think about that?

REPORTER: Do you have him?

ALI: Yea.

REPORTER: What's the date?

ALI: What date? December 2. Ah, we come to shock ya!!— (MUCH LAUGHER) We come to shock ya!!

REPORTER: How much do you plan to weigh when you fight?

ALI: I plan to weigh 230—yea, made a mistake comin' in with Holmes at 217. Had nothing—too dry, no strength.

REPORTER: How much do you weigh now?

ALI: 241—got eleven pounds.

REPORTER: How come you can't fight in the United States?

ALI: I can fight in Columbia, South Carolina. You know a strange thing that the so-called racist white people—so called bigoted states has always welcomed me first. Georgia during the draft time. Now Columbia, South Carolina—man I couldn't get no license in New York or Washington. Probably now they might.

REPORTER: Do you think you'll end up fighting in South Carolina?

ALI: We're working on it, yea.

REPORTER: How'd this, how'd this, come about? You went to them or they went to you or—

ALI: Well, we'd rather not go into that. I—know I

REPORTER: Why the Bahamas?

ALI: MMM well I like the Bahamas, nice weather. (LAUGHTER) Tourist tourist spot.

REPORTER: How many offers did you have before the Bahamas?

ALI: MMM

IJEOMA: You don't have to answer that!

ALI: Too many, but they wudn't they, wudn't in this country.

REPORTER: Muhammad, did you ever feel for a moment that your name may be exploited—somebody exploiting you because of your name?

ALI: Exploited me how? To promoted their country?

REPORTER: Yea, will . . .

ALI: That's good. It's an honor to say I can promote a whole country. (OVATION)—You know what I like? My real black power— I mean black power—I'm light power—He's (Cyril Ijeoma) black power!

REPORTER: Suppose Joe Frazier wanted to come back to fight? What is your reaction to this?

ALI: If he wanta come back—if he believe he can do it, it's his chance—he's taken a chance on going out worse than he came in— same as I am—it's all a chance—gamble. I heard somethin' once that says—He who is not courageous enough to take risks will accomplish nothing in life—get it now!—He who is not courageous enough to take risk will accomplish nothing in life. You know it takes a risky man to get on a rocket ship and go to another planet—anything could happen— know, know, know what encourages me also—I read about these four or five blind men climb a mountain twenty-five thousand feet high—I said how'd they find the way—a Braille map—what?! (LAUGHTER) Took a Braille map, no eye?! Somebody told you don't do it you'll get hurt—they say, no, we're gonna climb it—man I jumped up said, look a here let me make my come back here. (LAUGHTER) Another man ran across Canada on one peg leg more than I've ever run in my life 2,000 miles one on one—then died. Old Lady in Russia one hundred kickin' and dancin' (As Ali actually kicks, etc.) People stop too easy; people quit too easy. You know what the government should be doing— the government, the boxin commissions—with all the crime ya got in black comm—mm—black communities all the murder, all the killing, all the people who have no hope—I people love me—alot of these killers and gangsters love me and they see you trying to stop me from doing what I wanta do—they don't have no hope—hell! If he can't make it, what's the chance that I have? They should be encouraging me—Champ, come back—get in shape show 'em and don't be a quitter. You encourage all these youths and kids—go see what Muhammad Ali did—we told him he couldn't fight—we told the nigger you can't fight here—we took his license—we draw cartoons about him—we did everything to discourage him—he fought, he fought. He kept goin' and here he is—so let that be an example to you kid—don't stop because they tell you you can't do it. Too many people out there got problems and troubles—people tell you you can't do it. Odds against them, and they give up and lose hope—too many people lose hope and die. So I hope they can look at me and say look at Muhammad Ali—go on Ali! Handicapped people climbing mountains with one leg—they inspire me. And you goin' tell me I'm too old. Cartoons in the paper—bad at—making this guy named Bill Gallo, all kinda bad, suggestions old man with a beard and cane (as Ali makes noise and movement like old man on a cane) and you believe it if you keep listening to it. It made me get up and go quicker. I ran ten miles that day. (Ali laughs) I got one more thing to tell ya. Right here in America. Anybody here eighty years old? Do you know a lady eighty years old ran twenty-six miles? What? Running's hard as boxin—harder! Twenty-six miles—eighty years old. You, you do you think somebody told her she couldn't do it? I can't, I, I cannot do it today in four hours. I might die. She did twenty-six miles—she was 80—80—80 and you gona—her she ca— tell me I can't do it now. I'm too old? (LAUGHTER) Mannnnnn.

REPORTER: Will you fight in South Carolina before you fightin in the Bahamas?

ALI: Bahamas was the, was the first deal. REPORTER: Bahamas? ALI: Yea.

REPORTER: It's better in the Bahamas.

REPORTER: Have you been turned down for a license in New York?

ALI: A a a, witha, witha all the press we got here . . .

REPORTER: Were you turned down then?

ALI: Na, na, haven't tried—no, we didn't try. We I, I, I'd bet my life, bet my life that all the write-ups, all the press, and all the people lookin' out for my health and caring so much about me and loving me so much and after what Vegas turned me down—I'm sure they would here—New Yorks mmmmi— might have been the worst place to try cause . . .

REPORTER: What about Angelo? Angelo gona work with you in the corner with the same crew?

ALI: If he wants to—I know—he, he might not want to cause he's been one of the disbelievers.

REPORTER: Angelo has?

ALI: Yea.

REPORTER: He told me two weeks ago you looked greater than you ever did.

ALI: He did?

REPORTER: That's what he told me.

ALI: Oh! He heard I got that license—he heard I got that—did he? (LAUGHTER) Ol' Angelo's smart gettin his job back ain't he? (LAUGHTER)

REPORTER: Ali, are you making any kind of predictions on the upcoming fight?

ALI: No predictions.

REPORTER: What makes you and Berbick think that you'll draw, Ali?

ALI: I will draw! Don't need nobody else, I will draw!

REPORTER: It will be the DRAMA IN BAHAMAS!

ALI: THE DRAMA IN BAHAMAS. Hey man, you not as dumb as you look. (LAUGHTER) DRAMA IN BAHAMAS. Yea!

REPORTER: Cooney says he wants a tune-up fight with you.

ALI: Who wants a tune-up?

REPORTER: Cooney.

ALI: Cooney hits too hard. (LAUGHTER) Cooney hits so hard he'll jar yo' kin folk in Africa. Cooney's a good fella, too young.

REPORTER: Has Berbick agreed to fight you?

ALI: Huh?

REPORTER: Has Berbick agreed to fight you?

ALI: Has he?

REPORTER: Yea.

ALI: Yea.

REPORTER: Is it a signed contract or just your plan to fight him?

ALI: If not Ber—If not Berbick, I'd kinda like to . . .

REPORTER: Is there no signed contract with Berbick?

ALI: Naw, ah we ah we ah—what do we have?

IJEOMA: We have a verbal understanding with Berbick that he is willing to fight.

REPORTER: On what date?

IJEOMA: December 2. I spoke to him myself today.

ALI: If not Berbick, there's two more contenders, but they're, they're we're not gonna call, call—not put'em no pressure on they gotta sign real quick and get paid cause—they do it for the money.

REPORTER: What kinda money are you getting out of this?

ALI: My Lawyer'll tell ya. Where's my lawyer? Best lawyer in the country. He's got the connection and the complexion to get the protection. (LAUGHTER).

MICHAEL PHENNER: Well, I'm not gonna answer the question—best to say that Mr. Ali is satisfied with the money, and it's in the millions of dollars, but that's between the Internal Revenue Service and Mr. Ali as to the precise—we always report to the IRS.

REPORTER: Will you identify yourself please?

PHENNER: My name is Michael Phenner, and I'm Mr. Ali's attorney from Chicago.

REPORTER: Would you spell that please?

ALI: P-H-E-N-N-E-R.

REPORTER: When are they gonna start promoting?

ALI: We don't know—I predict that after they see when I get down to like 220 pounds and I'm lookin good and the press is writing— then they'll start promotin'.

REPORTER: How'd you like to fight Frazier again?

ALI: He's too old! (LAUGHTER)

DAVIS: With that—Ladies and Gentlemen—

ALI: I want, I want Frazier's son! (LAUGHTER)

DAVIS: With that Ladies and Gentlemen we'd like to thank you for coming and lending your support to this press conference. Thank you.

The press conference had gone extremely well. Ali was his usual self—jabbing and sparring with the reporters and photographers. Ali had handled himself well and demonstrated that he still had his flair for creating interest and controversy. Although an outside observer might have been turned off by the Champ's constant jabbering and mumbling, the veteran press and those of us who had followed Ali over the years saw the old glint in his eyes.

Ali was once again basking in the sunlight and enjoying every second. But underneath this facade, I could somehow sense some real trepidation and even a tinge of sadness in the Champ's voice. To me, he seemed to be trying to convince himself he could make this comeback, but he was deep down unsure of his abilities.

I doubt that anyone else felt this way, however, the reporters seemed to thoroughly enjoy the show, and Ali's usual entourage was more than pleased with this turn of events even though an outsider had made most of the arrangements.

The third "miracle" had now occurred, and that was all I could expect. After thousands of hours of toil, I had achieved, for all practical purposes, my ultimate goal.

In fact, I was just as excited about the outcome of the press conference as I would have been after the fight was over. The fight would merely be an anticlimax to all that had evolved in the past. This was the thrill of a lifetime! I jubilantly entered the elevator as Howard Bingham suddenly punched a guy in the mouth. (His record was now 2 and 0. His previous victory had come in Las Vegas against another loudmouth.)

Howard had warned Ali of the pimps and girls who would approach him and try to compromise the Champ. When Howard's predictions came true, Ali put an immediate stop to such activities.

Back in the hotel suite we were all jubilant from the successful press conference and laughter was in abundance. Ali, Phenner, Cyril and I slipped quietly into another room. As we sat down, the phone rang. Mike Phenner, Ali's attorney, answered the call. Don King wanted to know if he could do anything to help Ali. I was livid because of the brashness Don King had demonstrated with his phone call.

How on God's earth could he want to give assistance after telling the Champ that he would never help him into the ring again? I knew that he had the smell of green in his nostrils. When Mike handed the phone to Ali, I was unable to hear the full conversation, but I had no doubt that Don King was up to his old tricks and trying to worm his way into a piece of the action. Several days later Ali boarded a plane for Los Angeles. I had to stay in New York to work on the Berbick contract. On the day after Ali's departure, I met with the members of Sports Internationale Bahamas, Ltd. Edward C. Levine, who was not present, was represented by an attorney named Stern from a New York law firm. The meeting was abuzz with excitement and discussion about the fight. Since SI was an unknown to the rest of the world, we had to soothe everyone's ego. I had no idea the bomb was about to fall. While we were deciding on an opponent for Ali, someone asked about my background. I sensed a movement gathering momentum to force me to step aside as President of SI. I sketched out a brief resume and handed it to several individuals who were in effect, asking for my resignation. "Hell, no!" I adamantly declared. "I will not resign." I knew now that I would have to watch even my associates. Anyone familiar with boxing or any other professional sport knows that the business is cut-throat. It is not unusual for a supposedly close friend to figuratively stab a colleague in the back when big money appears on the horizon.

Any business can benefit from healthy competition, but the business of boxing is generally as rough and tumble as boxing itself. The only real difference is that it is far more difficult to get away with cheating in the ring than outside the ring. If every boxing match required the blood, sweat and tears of this one, the world would probably see no more than two or three heavyweight fights each decade.

I knew this fight would be worlds apart from any other and that the stakes were sky high. Ali would probably have the only chance any heavy-weight contender would ever have to be a four-time champion in my lifetime. And, if anyone could beat the record, Ali was the one.

Not being able to trust one's own friends is much akin to sleeping in the jungle—you never know when someone or something is going to tear you apart.

Whom do you trust and to what extent?

I hated like hell to face this situation for the next several days or even weeks, but once again, I had no choice. I must watch every word and every movement, lest someone have the opportunity to trip me.

We retired to our separate hotel rooms to reflect on the day's events. I was upset, but determined that I would not be squeezed out of the fight, particularly after I had faithfully performed all the preparatory work. Although we had announced at the press conference that Berbick would be Ali's opponent, Berbick still had not been signed. Of course, we had his verbal commitment.

The participants in the meeting reached a consensus that Berbick was the perfect opponent because of the 15 rounds he had gone against Larry Holmes.

On the next day I traveled to Kennedy Airport to meet Berbick's flight from Canada. As Trevor walked down the runway, I was awed by his physical build and I wondered if we had chosen the right opponent. He was represented by Sam Glass, a New York promoter-manager. After a runaround from LaBreque, we finally had Trevor in our hands along with a legitimate representative. As the meeting began, I sensed that we would have difficulty signing Berbick. His demand of half a million dollars was absurd. Don King Productions paid him only $110,000 for his title fight in Las Vegas with Larry Holmes.

The meeting soon reached a stalemate. I could not in good conscience offer Berbick that kind of money. Ed was so excited about this event, but he had to realize such a payment would be suicide. We talked to our partners in Nassau, and Frankie's idea was the best: invite Trevor and Glass to Nassau and, maybe, a change of scenery would stimulate a signed contract.

I boarded a flight back to Los Angeles to meet with Paul and my attorneys and more importantly, to obtain some money. Paul had reserved dinner at Scandia and he and Richard were waiting at the bar when I arrived. I received my usual hero's welcome from Paul. I spoke privately with John and asked for $25,000. I made no promises that a deal had been made, but I felt my Bahamian partners could trust me. John could trust me. He had to discuss my need with Lionel Shane, Vice President of Select TV, but he saw no major obstacles.

My nerves were on edge. Paul and I had written bad checks all over Los Angeles, and my fears grew that some snoopy reporter would track me down and blow the whole project. "Sports promotion President arrested for bad checks," the headlines would proclaim.

I had to have the money to pay the bills. My fears grew as I worked daily on the promotion and came home at night to face the music.

Eviction could come any day. Although very fearful that word had gotten spread and I would be discovered a fugitive from Atlanta, I had to take my chances and go on promoting the fight. 1 took as many precautions as I could to avoid being tracked down and arrested, but I realized I would have to face the music, sooner or later. If I could only postpone my ultimate fate until after the match, I believed I could accept the consequences. For now, however, I had to continue to elude the FBI and any other authorities who had reason to be pursuing me. Every time I heard the doorbell buzz or a phone ring, I would jump about two feet, fearful that this was my last moment of freedom.

Whenever feasible, I asked my wife to answer the door, or whenever I was away from home, I recruited friends and acquaintances to screen my visitors and phone calls.

If I were arrested before the fight, I would have no choice but to either hope that the parties would honor the contract and deliver my full share to me or that I would be immediately released on bail (assuming I could post bond) so I could oversee the operation.

Since I had deliberately severed all communications with Atlanta, I had no idea on whether I was a wanted man and, if so, who wanted me?

Eventually, I would be caught since I had left a trail of cold checks along the way that was certain to lead to my arrest. The investigations and paperwork are time-consuming for banks and authorities in check fraud cases, and thus time could be on my side at this point.

John and Lionel agreed to loan me $25,000. When I received the first check, I promised to repay the loan from proceeds of the fight regardless of whether or not a cable contract was executed. Thanks to funds from Select and Medallion TV, I once again honored bad checks, paid old bills and repaid Paul and my attorneys.

The Minister was due in town within two days and so everything would have to be down pat. Paul and his friend Gito and I went to Beverly Hills to rent a car. My Bahamian partners were coming to Los Angeles, and I could not pick them up at LAX in the Pinto. I had hocked my own car the month before to pay bills and buy food and other essential goods. I waited at the Los Angeles airport in a shiny blue Mercedes for Franklyn Wilson, Vice President of S.I.B.L. and Mr. Kendall Nottage, Minister of Youth, Sports and Community Affairs. They arrived late at night, and since my guests appeared very tired, we talked very little. We met the next morning to discuss business.

Paul had made reservations for Mr. Nottage and Mr. Wilson at the Beverly Hilton. When we met in the morning, the Minister seemed upset. He was extremely angry.

Had I done something wrong? Our discussions intensified as we focused on pro-rated revenues for the Broadcasting Corporation of the Bahamas. I thought Paul had performed magnificently under the circumstances.

In our meeting with Select TV in the law offices of Paul Caruso in Beverly Hills there were at least 45 individuals. First, Mr. Nottage expressed his concern that certain monies were being provided to the Broadcasting Corporation. This issue could kill the contract, but since we were not in America, any radio or TV that was broadcast would have to be approved by the Bahamian Broadcasting Corporation. The negotiations continued into the late evening, thanks to compromise after compromise and offer after counteroffer.

We finally recessed for dinner at Scandia. When we returned to the hotel, everyone seemed exhausted. Finally, I had a free moment to see the Champ who had been working out every day while waiting for training camp to start in Nassau and to say hello to my family.

But the negotiations were to continue although the Minister had to depart to Nassau. Paul stayed in Los Angeles to work with the cable companies. I had allowed him to use my guest bedroom at Arden.

For once, I said goodbye to my wife with all the bills paid. Every time I had to leave my wife and sons, I would get the eerie feeling that this "goodbye" could be the last one.

This time, however, I felt a bit more comfortable since, for the moment at least, my creditors were satisfied and my utility payments were up-to-date. There was also some liquid cash, which my wife could use for groceries and other essentials. I had spent so little time with my family that I wondered if they even recognized me. This fight had absorbed so much of my time for so long that it had become more than an obsession—it had become my life and even my livelihood. If this battle somehow did not materialize, my career was surely doomed.

My optimism now was at its peak though, everything pointed toward successful execution of this project, including the tacit assumptions on the part of all parties (the lawyers, the investors, the Bahamian government and Ali and supposedly Berbick) that only the minor details remained to be ironed out.

I felt great, probably better than I had felt in a long time. Once this deal was finalized and the fight was over, I planned to briefly celebrate and then break for a long rest. I needed the time to rejuvenate and, most of all, be with my family with whom I had almost become estranged. It would take some time to convince my wife I was her husband and my sons that I was indeed their father.

Before leaving California for New York and on to Nassau for training, I made one last attempt to convince the world that the fight was for real. Jim Hill, a close friend of the Champ's interviewed Ali on a television show. When questions arose about Ali's poor showing against Larry Holmes, I introduced opinions from the UCLA medical team. Maybe just maybe, this evidence would be sufficient to convince everyone that Ali had been treated for the wrong ailment in this bout. Maybe these medical records would put to rest the rumors about his general health and brain damage.

Sunday night at LAX was utter chaos with more friends, well-wishers, and helpers boarding the flight to New York for more fireworks. This time we would check into the Summit Hotel after an eventful flight during which Dick Shapp of ABC Sports expressed his concerns about Ali entering the ring again.

Our Summit Hotel press conference began with Ali taunting the press about black children needing black heroes. Then shock waves traveled down my spine—Ali finally told the world how this event had evolved: "Ladies and Gentlemen of the press, I wanna introduce a young man who has traveled all over the world. A young man who got me the license to fight again. I bring on James Cornelius." I bowed and immediately sat down. The press conference ended with all of us at Sports Internationale jubilant that Ali had effectively manipulated the press.

CHAPTER SIX

When we all retired to one of the suites, the question on all our minds was: What was Nassau like?

I had traveled the length of the United States four times but had been to Nassau for only brief visits.

I boarded our flight for Nassau. We chided Howard during the whole trip. Nassau International Airport was the happiest place on earth with thousands of people chanting, "Ali, Ali, ALI." Even the Commonwealth broadcasting network showed up.

What a welcome for the Champ!

The next day was business as usual. We began with the work permits. Each fighter, cook, masseur, trainer; etc. connected with this fight had to have a work permit. Cyril and I visited the Commonwealth's Police Headquarters where many of the applications for temporary work permits had to be checked to detect any prior criminal records. My record stretched back some 20 years, and so Cyril spoke privately with the deputy police commissioner, who happened to be his brother-in-law.

After brief introductions, we were escorted to one of the commanding officers units.

My nerves were on edge. I wondered if they had learned the FBI was looking for me. As I paced the floor, I noticed a folder on the desk that appeared to be linked to some sort of investigation. Did the information concern me? When I opened the folder I noticed Robert Vesco's name along with some type of investigative report on drugs.

Before I could read further, I heard footsteps and closed the folder. Sweat formed on my brows as I quickly sat down.

I began to conceive a plan to avoid being arrested and possibly extradited to the United States. I would simply convince the Nassau officials that the FBI must be mistakenly looking for me since I had done nothing more than commit some innocent blunders that somehow had managed to get blown all out of proportion. I could assure the Bahamian government that, if I were allowed to remain free until after the fight, I could then clear up all of the confusion. "Please allow me to see this fight to its culmination," I would plead, "and I promise to Almighty God I will answer for any sins I may have committed."If this plan failed, I would have to consider the possibility of eluding Nassau police until the fight was over. I was not sure how this could be accomplished, but I realized I had to seriously consider this alternative.

By now I was literally sitting on the edge of my chair, anxiously awaiting Cyril's return. My agony was exacerbated by the fact that Cyril was gone for several minutes. "Surely he would have come back by now," I thought. "If there were no problems, why was he taking so long?"

My past was proving to be more and more of an anathema. I was not free to travel anywhere anymore, even in a country as far removed from nowhere as the Bahamas. Staying out of the limelight and away from the authorities who were pursuing me was becoming an impossible task.

My heart pounded with excitement, but I was extremely relieved when Cyril indicated my work permit had been approved.

Two weeks later Drew and Blood told me Ali was making good progress both in and out of the ring. Even his longtime cook Lana said Ali was doing well. Michael Phenner, Ali's Chicago attorney, called to inform us of a prior commitment that the Champ had in Hong Kong, where he was to appear on October 10. Ali, at 39, needed this break in training as much as he needed a hole in the head.

Either we had to call off the fight or move it back to late December. Since money was in short supply and there was bickering about building the stadium, I had to delay this decision.

Ali's plane would return through the Pacific, with a stopover in Los Angeles.

This change of pace would work out perfectly since Ali could hold a press conference at the Beverly Wilshire Hotel, providing a big promotional boost for the fight.

Select TV and Shelly Saltman, co-promoters of the event, had planned a big press conference, but the timing was bad. The Los Angeles Dodgers were winning the World Series, killing any hopes of a large turnout at the conference.

I called Herbert in Chicago to tell him that Ali was upset because his friend Don King had threatened to wreck the show if he didn't get $150,000 in cash. I immediately called Mr. King and promised him the money since I knew he had the ability to carry out his threats.

I left S. Arden on time in the limo to pick up the Champ to transport him to the press conference. Ali complained all the way down that we had scheduled the conference at a bad time. "Everyone is gonna be at City Hall with Mayor Bradley and the Dodgers," Ali contended.

"Champ, there is nothing in sports as popular as you, or even in the world," I countered. "Just wait and see." Even I had doubts about the veracity of my statement.

I was shocked as I entered the room. It was overflowing with every major network and wire service there, as well as the local media.

Who was covering the Dodgers? The podium was filled with champions including Ali, Thomas "Hitman" Hernes, Greg Page and Trevor Berbick. Fred Stirrup, an outstanding sportswriter from Nassau had even arranged a satellite hookup for Nassau.

The press conference went extremely well with Ali taking center stage. Ali displayed a degree of confidence I had not seen for some time. Except for his physical appearance, Ali was very much like the Champ of his heydays.

Ali was cocky and yet firm with the reporters. He reiterated his intention to defeat Berbick as a demonstration of his inner and outer strength.

Berbick, according to the Champ, was merely a minor roadblock to a glorious comeback—a comeback that would signal to the world that what seems impossible is possible when it comes to Muhammad Ali.

Although some of the reporters' questions bordered on commentary, in light of their skeptical tone, Ali had no problem laying to rest all of the rumors regarding his mental and physical condition.

The champ was clearly ready for his bout and diplomatically lambasted the press for its lack of conviction and confidence that he would win.

Ali always provided good copy for the press in his outspoken and sincere statements and answers, and this "confrontation" was no exception.

The Champ had conducted enough press conferences like this one to make him an experienced and effective communicator. Ali always displayed that necessary human touch in his meetings with the press, often citing individual journalists by name, whether or not he or she had treated him favorably in the past. What a show!

The day after the conference we flew back to Nassau.

Beverly Hills' Press Conference, l-r, Cyril Ijeoma, Ali, and James Cornelius. Photo supplied by Howard Bingham.

Ali at press conference, Beverly Wilshire Hotel, Beverly Hills, CA, l-r, James Cornelius with Ali. Photo supplied by Howard Bingham.

Beverly Hills' Press Conference, l-r James Cornelius, the Champ, David Gardner & Tommy Hearns. Photo supplied by Howard Bingham.

Beverly Hills' Press Conference, l-r Heavyweight Champ, Greg Page, Muhammad Ali, Canadian Heavyweight Champ, Trevor Berbick, World Welterweight Champion, Tommy "Hit Man" Hearns. Photo supplied by Howard Bingham.

CHAPTER SEVEN

Photographed at Ali's Last Training Camp, The Cabaret Theater,
Britannia Beach Hotel, Paradise Island, Nassau, Bahamas.
Photographs taken and supplied by Brenda Foye Cornelius.

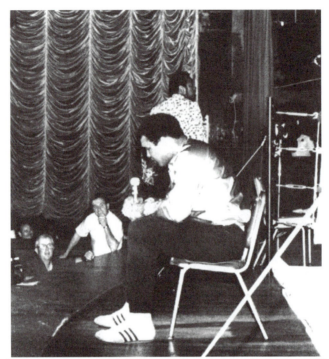

Photographed at Ali's Last Training Camp, The Cabaret Theater,

Britannia Beach Hotel, Paradise Island, Nassau, Bahamas.

Photographs taken and supplied by Brenda Foye Cornelius.

Photographed at Ali's Last Training Camp, The Cabaret Theater,
Britannia Beach Hotel, Paradise Island, Nassau, Bahamas.
Photographs taken and supplied by Brenda Foye Cornelius.

Photographed at Ali's Last Training Camp, The Cabaret Theater,
Britannia Beach Hotel, Paradise Island, Nassau, Bahamas.
Photographs taken and supplied by Brenda Foye Cornelius.

Photographed at Ali's Last Training Camp, The Cabaret Theater,
Britannia Beach Hotel, Paradise Island, Nassau, Bahamas.
Photographs taken and supplied by Brenda Foye Cornelius.

Photographed at Ali's Last Training Camp, The Cabaret Theater,

Britannia Beach Hotel, Paradise Island, Nassau, Bahamas.

Photographs taken and supplied by Brenda Foye Cornelius.

Photographed at Ali's Last Training Camp, The Cabaret Theater,
Britannia Beach Hotel, Paradise Island, Nassau, Bahamas.
Photographs taken and supplied by Brenda Foye Cornelius.

Photographed at Ali's Last Training Camp, The Cabaret Theater,
Britannia Beach Hotel, Paradise Island, Nassau, Bahamas.
Photographs taken and supplied by Brenda Foye Cornelius.

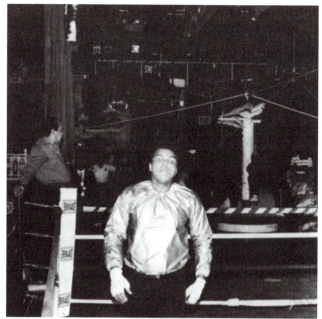

Photographed at Ali's Last Training Camp, The Cabaret Theater,
Britannia Beach Hotel, Paradise Island, Nassau, Bahamas.
Photographs taken and supplied by Brenda Foye Cornelius.

Photographed at Ali's Last Training Camp, The Cabaret Theater,
Britannia Beach Hotel, Paradise Island, Nassau, Bahamas.
Photographs taken and supplied by Brenda Foye Cornelius.

Photographed at Ali's Last Training Camp, The Cabaret Theater,
Britannia Beach Hotel, Paradise Island, Nassau, Bahamas.
Photographs taken and supplied by Brenda Foye Cornelius.

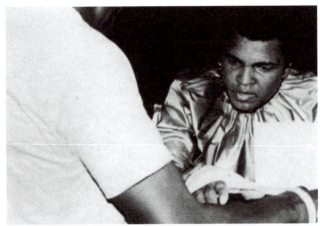

Photographed at Ali's Last Training Camp, The Cabaret Theater,
Britannia Beach Hotel, Paradise Island, Nassau, Bahamas.
Photographs taken and supplied by Brenda Foye Cornelius.

We had been encamped in the swank Britannia Beach Hotel since September 21, 1981. The hotel had been generous in extending credit and granting allotments to some of the entourage, but the hotel managers finally asked me to meet with them because the entourage had exceeded its daily allotment for food and the dry cleaning and overseas phone bills were past due. Even our liquor bills were out of sight.

George Meyers, the hotel's chief executive, wanted some form of payment. He had been very accommodating up to now, but his patience had subsided. When we presented him with about $10,000, some of his pain seemed to have been soothed.

The next problem that arose was completing the stadium facilities. The building materials had to come from Miami and yet the fight was only 19 days away. To make matters worse, Ali had discontinued training because he had not received a $100,000 payment, and there were no funds to pay him.

It was Tuesday, November 17, and time was flying. I tried to keep tabs on the progress of Ali's training through daily contact with his trainers. Ali's October trip to Hong Kong had cost us ten days of valuable training. At age 39 Ali could ill afford to lose one moment of daily training.

I met Ali in his dressing room offstage of the hotel cabaret room, where luscious beauties danced by night for the amusement of Casino goers. The room served by day as Ali's training camp. Ali cleared the room of his personnel so that we could confer privately. When he skinned off his trunks I was stunned by his magnificent physique and wondered how many women would like to grasp this tremendous hunk. While barely rearing his head, Ali told me, "Ya 'know, Cornelius, promoting is hard stuff. Suppose someone put $200,000 in a briefcase for you and you forgot about this fight."

I could see Don King's handiwork in Ali's statement. Everyone seemed to be closing in for the kill. Don King had applied pressure on Herbert, Ali's Manager, and now Herbert was applying pressure on Ali. Grasping for words, I simply responded, "Champ, I'll see you later." I thought about Ali's statement and realized that the $100,000 was now a real obstacle. Obviously someone was standing in the wings waiting to pick up the tab. After all I had gone through; the Champ was now asking me to give up. The fight was so close to fruition now. The Bahamian government had gone above and beyond the call of duty, at my insistence, when everyone else in the world had not only denied Ali a license to box again, but had attempted to deter the Bahamian government from granting a license. I owed something to the people of Nassau. I couldn't quit now.

Somehow I would have to convince Ali that his money would be forthcoming and thus that he should remain in Nassau. I knew that if Ali ever left Nassau, there would be no fight.

I gathered my partners in my suite and explained the situation. We all agreed that it would be disastrous for Ali to leave the island. Jeremiah Shabazz, a long-time Ali friend and adviser, and Abdul Rahman spoke at different times to Ali trying to convince him of the necessity to stay in Nassau. I decided to wait until after their pleas before I would confront the Champ again. After I received word that the meetings had been held, I went to the Champ's suite. When I realized Ali was on the long distance phone, I knew I had to choose my words carefully. Above all else, I had to convince Ali to stay in Nassau. I had never been more determined than now that this fight would take place. Finally, Ali ended the conversation with the party on the other end.

I had prepared my speech. I knew that the Champ was concerned about the $100,000 payment, but I would behave as if it were a foregone conclusion that he would be paid. I began our discussion by telling him how it was unfair for him to stop training this close to the fight. At his age, I contended, every second of training is valuable. My statement struck a nerve!

Ali jumped to his feet and said, "Nigger, I'm the boss.

83

You ain't never promoted a fight before."

I suppressed my hurt and said, "Champ, you're right; you are the boss, but nobody on earth was willing to help you but me at the time you needed help." Then I left the room.

I had made my point and if Ali chose to act against me now, I would simply have to live with that fact. I had made a good faith effort to meet all of my commitments to Ali, and I had every intention of securing the $100,000 I had promised.

Although I may have been guilty of putting forth less than my best in the past, this fight had almost literally consumed me. It had occupied almost every waking moment and forced me to make enormous financial and personal sacrifices for which I was unlikely to ever be compensated.

As much as I loved and respected the Champ, I saw this last contact with him as the last opportunity to show him that we deserved each other's respect and trust and even, perhaps, admiration.

I sincerely believed that I had provided Ali with his very last opportunity to prove all the skeptics and all the historians wrong. Ali was not infallible, but if he could pull this one off (and I strongly believed he could), he would surely become America's greatest legend.

I must admit that, at the moment, legends were not my primary concern. I was concerned; above all else, that Ali would get advice from the wrong people and blow this deal to bits and pieces. Men of the stature of the Champ necessarily rely upon a coterie of individuals for constant advice and counsel, but all too often, such friends and companions offer wrong advice. I have learned that it is easy to counsel someone on what to do when you do not have to personally accept the consequences.

I had to raise that money quickly. My back was to the wall. I decided to sell some stock and was told that Tee Kay Bahamas, a shipping company, would be interested in purchasing a part of Sports Internationale Bahamas, Ltd.

(SIBL) The negotiations were difficult and very intense, but we finally settled on a purchase price of $300,000, which was just enough to pay Ali's $100,000 and pay some of the outstanding debts such as the equipment in Miami. Most of my interest in SIBL was gone now, and I even had to loan the company $40,000 of the proceeds.

I had mixed emotions about Ali's trying to fight after such poor preparation, especially in light of his age.

I will never forget Monday, November 23, 1981. Ali appeared at a press conference in the heart of Bay Street, and Trafalgar Square to announce that the fight was on and that he was satisfied with the financial arrangements. Now the whole world knew—Ali will fight Berbick! I can never forget how "Blood", Ali's long-time trainer, and I eyed each other during the press conference, as though we'd never forget this island paradise.

While "Blood" was a long-time companion and confidant of Ali, and I was merely the new kid on the block, we had a lot in common. We were both concerned about Ali's physical and mental condition for the fight, and yet we knew the fight had to occur. Too many individuals, including the two of us, had devoted a horrendous amount of time, effort and even money for things to go awry.

The eyes of the United States and indeed the world were now focused on the Bahamas. There were still a few details to be resolved such as the intricate financial arrangements but, barring an act of God, the fight was destined to take place December 11.

The Ali-Berbick match was receiving enormous publicity, both in the United States and in the Bahamas. Front-page stories and photographs were the norm, especially as the date for the fight drew closer.

Much of the press coverage was critical of Ali, especially for trying a comeback at age 39 and for not, as they viewed it, getting himself into top mental and physical condition. But even negative publicity is better than no publicity. The more people heard about the controversy, the more likely they were to buy a ticket to view the fight on closed-circuit television. Every dollar of revenue would count since it would be applied toward paying off the huge outstanding loans.

No one, especially promoters, wants to lose money!

The United States Embassy in Nassau had gotten involved in this event and mailed invitations for a reception in honor of Muhammad Ali. The stage was set for Ali to be paid tribute by the United States government.

What a pleasure to see one of America's great heroes receiving this attention! We had been invited to be on board the destroyer DuPoint, a Naval vessel docked in Bahamian waters. When boarded, we were given a first class tour by its Commander. As we approached the deck where the crew had been assembled by the top brass, the Commander handed me two Naval caps and asked me if the Champ could put one on.

I walked over to the microphone where Ali was about to address the men and handed him the cap. He took it and pulled it down over his short crop. A feeling went through me that was unexplainable. Ali looked out at the men and said, "Ya know they tried to get me on one of these things once." (The men all laughed.) He then said very seriously, "Fight for your Country." He sparred a few rounds with a couple of men, and we departed. Ali had always been a true champion. Even when his country had chosen to persecute him for his religious convictions, he had not been bitter.

Ali was devoted to Allah since he had dedicated his life to the Muslim religion, but he also held a deep loyalty to his country. The Champ would never criticize the United States even when the government was pressing to prosecute him for refusing to be drafted. I found this difficult to comprehend, but I'm sure Ali has his reasons.

When the Champ placed that cap on his head, his symbolic gesture struck a responsive chord among all of the men.

These men, even though most of their beliefs were probably at odds with Ali's religious and political beliefs, saw the Champ as a man of convictions—a man who was unafraid to speak his mind but who also had a deep and abiding respect and even understanding of the beliefs and feelings of others.

Their laughter and applause were as spontaneous as Ali's gesture and symbolized that all was right with the world at that given moment.

I was pleased to have provided Ali with the opportunity to show his compassion and understanding at a time when most of the world had some doubt about Ali's fate on December 11.

U.S. Embassy Reception, Muhammad Ali with U.S. Charge d'Affaires, Andrew F. Antippas. Photo supplied by Howard Bingham.

U.S. Embassy Reception, Nassau, Bahamas, Muhammad Ali and the Honorable Senator Kendall W. Nottage. Photo supplied by Howard Bingham.

U.S. Embassy Reception, the Champ with unidentified guest. Photo supplied by Howard Bingham.

U.S. Embassy Reception, Nassau, Bahamas, l-r, Veronica Ali, the Champ, James Cornelius, Brenda Cornelius, The Honorable Senator Kendall W. Nottage and his wife Ruby Nottage. Photo supplied by Howard Bingham.

U.S. Embassy Reception, Nassau, Bahamas, l-r, James Cornelius, Cassius Clay Sr., Veronica Ali, the Champ. Photo supplied by Howard Bingham.

*U.S. Embassy Reception. The Honorable Kendall W. Nottage, Ms.
Ruby Nottage, James & Brenda Cornelius. Photo supplied by
Howard Bingham.*

I left the ship to find Charles Major. Negotiations with our new group had broken down and I knew I must call the Prime Minister since Charles was responsible for keeping our progress. When I found Charles and told him of the news, he was shocked but agreed to drive me to within a few blocks of the Prime Minister's residence. Charles refused to drive any closer, but I did not mind walking a few blocks. We took the scenic drive down Cable Beach, and all during the trip Charles kept saying, "Mystery man, you are crazy!" I could focus my thoughts only on seeing this project through.

As I approached the house, the Royal Guards looked rather unfriendly with their submachine guns.

How could I possibly talk my way in to see the Prime Minister?

After some soul-searching, I concluded that I faced an insurmountable roadblock. I abandoned my plans and headed for Blue Hill Road. Maybe I could get "Nine" to call for me. He agreed and when the telephone rang, and he answered, I quickly apologized to the Prime Minister for bothering him at home.

"Mr. Prime Minister, this is James Cornelius," I said, "One of the promoters of the fight. I can't get Mr. Wilson and Mr. Ijeoma to cooperate." (Silence) Then in his British-Bahamian accent, he responded. "You can't do what?"

"Well, sir, they are just not giving me any help."

"Get this thing done."

"Yes Sir!"

Prime Minister Lindling O. Pindling, and Muhammad Ali. Photo supplied by Howard Bingham.

Prime Minister Lindling O. Pindling, and Muhammad Ali. Photo supplied by Howard Bingham.

l-r, Prime Minister, Lindling O. Pindling, Charles Major, Jr., James Cornelius watch the Champ autograph "T"-shirts. Photo supplied by Howard Bingham.

The Champ and members of Sports Internationale, Bahamas Limited visit with Prime Minister Lindling O. Pindling, l-r, James Cornelius, Prime Minister Lindling O. Pindling, the Champ, Charles Major, Jr., & Frank Wilson. Photo supplied by Howard Bingham.

Members of Sports Internationale, Bahamas Limited, leaving Government House, Nassau, Bahamas, l-r, James Cornelius, Frank Wilson, Veronica Ali, and the Champ. Photo supplied by Howard Bingham.

Ali and Veronica visit with Millie, a Bahamian native. Photo supplied by Howard Bingham.

Ali, with Veronica and Cornelius looking on, demonstrates how he plans to take Berbick out. Photo supplied by Howard Bingham.

Charles Major, Jr. with Bahamians outside Government House.

Photo supplied by Howard Bingham.

Ali and Veronica cavort with Bahamians. Photo supplied by Howard Bingham.

CHAPTER EIGHT

Ali's personal manager, Herbert Muhammad, had flown in to be with the Champ. Ali, accompanied by Herbert and me, paid a courtesy call to the Bahamas Youth and Sports Ministry. The Bahamian television network covered the event live. We were warmly welcomed by the head of the Ministry, who praised Ali for his commitment to and support of youth around the world. We deliberately kept the ceremony brief since there were important issues to be settled. Don King had injected himself in the promotion of the fight by claiming that he was entitled to promote Berbick because of a contract in which he and Berbick had entered following the Berbick-Holmes fight.

Because of the media attention, we met with the Minister and discussed King's involvement. I really wanted a face-to-face meeting with all the parties so the Don King controversy could be resolved, once and for all.

I did not feel Don King was entitled to any proceeds from this fight, but, obviously, his demands could throw a monkey wrench into the whole affair. I would do whatever was necessary to clear the air.

The Youth Minister was concerned about Don King's request for money. Herbert Muhammad agreed with my view but added that Don King was not a man who could be ignored.

The Youth Minister's eyes burned with indignation.

"What makes him think that he can come here and take $200,000 from Sports Internationale, Ltd?" he asked.

Exhausted from all of the media attention and legal sparring, Ali suggested, "Why don't I put $50,000 from my purse in a pot and let Sports Internationale, Ltd. put up another $50,000?" I knew that would get Don King off our backs, but I realized that the Champ seriously believed that Don King had the ability to destroy the fight.

Although I was furious now, I refused to allow my anger to show. This meeting had at least one clear outcome: everyone said I should pay off Don King.

Cyril, one of the partners in Sports Internationale, sat very quietly during the entire discussion. I was glad that he was present because the other partners were outraged that I had Okayed a payoff to King. I simply could not allow Don to stop this affair, and under the circumstances, I had no choice but to agree to the payoff.

Don King is a man that anyone must take seriously. Whether or not he felt he had a legitimate right to the money (i.e. a binding contract that would hold up in court) was irrelevant. He was in a position to make the demand, and I believed he was perfectly capable of carrying out his threats.

The Don King controversy was a new impediment, but I had become accustomed by now to obstacles of every sort from the financial to the political and from the unusual to the bizarre.

The real question was whether King would settle for an amount equal to half of that demanded or whether he would press hard for the full $200,000. I could merely guess about his strategy, but I had a sneaking suspicion that even if King accepted the $100,000, we would not be seeing the last of him. King always had a way of popping up at crucial moments, and his timing in this case was perfect since the project was more vulnerable than it had ever been.

Moments like this are when I have the greatest difficulty controlling my anger. If I ever needed the patience of Job, now was the time. Fortunately, I held back my anger and engaged in some rational thinking. What would be King's response? What was likely to be his next step?

The Youth Minister and Herbert Muhammad agreed that I had been truthful with everyone and were assured that I was not trying to rip off Sports Internationale Bahamas, Ltd.

We all knew that King's demands were serious.

Nothing was resolved at the meeting, but at least the Champ and Herbert were convinced that King would not sit idly by.

Monday, December 7, was marked by fury and anger when a shoving match broke out between Bundini and me. Since I had to pick up the expenses for the entourage, I had continually and consistently asked Ali to hold the expenditures of the entourage within certain budgetary restrictions.

My words had obviously fallen on deaf ears. The hotel was pressing for payment, and I did not have the money available. Something had to give. The members of the entourage simply would not restrain themselves.

The result was a shoving and shouting match between Bundini and me. We needed money and Tee Kay Bahamas, which had loaned us $300,000 just three weeks before, would not offer more. I remained level-headed attending all of the meetings and keeping appointments with the fighters. I also appeared at the new offices since I felt it necessary to keep up staff morale. I urgently needed to meet with my business partners to determine the progress they had made in raising additional funds.

I had not heard from them during the last few days. Thus I would have to go to Centerville House, where they were working if I wanted to meet with them.

As I had done so often before, I rode the slim elevator up to their floor and exited. This time, however, I found all of the doors open, a rather unusual situation, especially at this time of night.

As I cautiously walked down the hallway, I overheard what I thought were telephone conversations.

Was I losing my mind? Was my partner, Ijeoma, talking to Don King with Frankie listening? Were my partners selling me out behind my back?

I listened a little longer and realized that with all the sophisticated telephone devices on the market, they were actually on a speaker phone. As I surreptitiously listened to the conversation, I learned that the Larry Holmes-Renaldo Snipes fight had been a total disappointment to the fans. Suddenly an idea flashed in my mind!

Because of my problems with the FBI, I had avoided re-entering the United States before the fight. Now Don King was demanding $200,000 from me. I had been lax enough to provide Don King with the perfect opportunity to infiltrate the company. I had asked Ijeoma, whom I trusted, to attend the fight in my place.

Don King had seized the perfect opportunity. Now my partners were dealing behind my back!

My heart sank to my feet when I comprehended the direction this project had taken. Although I had been desperate many times in the past, this conversation was the first indication that matters were now out of hand.

I could no longer trust anyone with whom I was dealing. Even my cohorts would be suspect, now that the stakes were so high and now that I could no longer deal in good faith.

To whom should I now place my loyalties? I could never take comfort in ever having to betray anyone, but I had to get to the bottom of this matter, one way or another.

Even in the dog-eat-dog world of boxing, one has to be able to place his trust and faith in someone—you cannot strike out on your own.

But whom could I trust now that I had lost confidence in my partners? Do I continue as though I were unaware of these wheelings and dealings or do I directly confront them?

There is an old saying that information is power. Now that I was familiar with these new developments, perhaps I could use the knowledge to my advantage and spring a trap when the mice least expected one.

However the stakes may have changed, my strategy now had to take into account that my partners were not necessarily on my side. I was dealing from a stacked deck.

CHAPTER NINE

By Tuesday, December 8, three days before the fight, all of my attempts to find funds had failed. I was weary as I entered Frankie's office, where I found he and Cyril drafting a telex to Michael Phenner, Ali's attorney. Shirley was standing at the telex machine with that old familiar look that hinted something was wrong. I calmed myself and softly told Cyril that I felt the need for a conference before the telex was transmitted. This fight was too important to be cancelled. We were so close now. A decision had been made to send the wire canceling the fight without ever consulting me.

My anger increased and I must have broken the sound barrier when I said, "Gentlemen, we have many hours of work in this fight and I hope that you will at least hear me out before canceling the fight."

I then explained slowly that I had found someone with the $150,000 we needed to make the fight happen.

Groping for words, I finally said, "I hope you can find the strength to hold on for one more day."

Cyril would certainly agree to an extension.

Having just returned from a secluded weekend, I convinced the group that I had found the money in the United States.

Now, all I had left to do was to lend truth to the lie.

I left the office that afternoon and went straight to my suite to find my phone ringing off the hook with calls from all over the world. My assistant, who handled overseas communications with reporters and others, was in Los Angeles. Thanks to these calls, my suite was a madhouse. In order to enjoy peace and quiet, I decided to have dinner in the hotel dining room instead of my suite. I desperately needed to collect my thoughts.

Lying is always the easy task. The difficulty comes when one has to prove the lie is true.

I was in a desperate position as usual, with nowhere to go and no one to whom I could turn. $150,000 is a chunk of dough, but I had to procure it and more somewhere soon.

The toil and trouble this project had brought me were now beginning to take their toll. I was feeling extremely tried, even exhausted, and often I felt confused. I became so absorbed in arriving at a solution to this problem of securing financing that I frequently bumped into individuals and even walls and other objects without realizing what I was doing.

My mental state was nearing a total wreck with only strains of sanity remaining to hold me together.

I really had no serious doubts about eventually pulling through with a successful execution of the project, but I saw extremely rough times ahead. I concentrated every waking moment, which was almost 24 hours a day since I never seem to be able to turn off my worries long enough to fall asleep, to the fight. I could see Ali trouncing Berbick, while I sat in sheer joy on the sidelines, knowing that I had made history possible.

Even if my name were never mentioned again in connection with this fight, I could delight in the fact that I was the crucial factor in making it possible.

I was so engrossed in thought that when the elevator quickly reached a floor, I stepped briskly down the hallway, stuck my key in the lock and discovered I had gotten off on the wrong floor. As I started for the elevator, I spotted Victor Sayyah, who represented a group of prospective investors. Victor and I had discussed for several days the possible involvement of the group but without success. Maybe fate was on my side. I asked Victor if we could talk, and we agreed to go to the lobby for a drink. Since we chose a bar close to the casino, we had to talk amidst the clank and clatter of slot machines and the noise of patrons talking about the big fight. Victor was a handsome man with keen features. He had a small scar on the right side of his face, which was enough to dispel any thoughts I might have about deceiving him. As we talked I sensed the gentleness of this man and found him incredibly straightforward. He surmised that my CPA partners were not playing with a full deck, a conclusion that I had already reached. I convinced Victor that, with $450,000, I could make the "Drama in the Bahamas" happen. To my complete surprise, he agreed to work with me beginning the next day. The last miracle had taken place and the pieces were falling into place. But had I overlooked anything? Were there any other potential obstacles?

The press was generally critical of the fight. Even worse, as I had been warned by friends and colleagues, media attention to this event was sparse. Patty, our press agent, and Dick Young of New York seemed to be the only individuals with a sense of fairness. Contracts and money were now delivered to every fighter on the card. I had a local artist paint the canvas that displayed the symbols of Sports Internationale Bahamas, Ltd. (SIBL) Although Select TV pressured me to sell the canvas to an advertiser for $75,000, I refused since, to me, this work of art represented the pride of six men and, more importantly, the pride of a whole nation.

We had moved our offices from Laventhol, Horwrath to the office of Bahamas World Airlines since Victor was accustomed to working there. Tickets were finally being sold and we were now ready for the big press conference and weigh-in on Thursday.

Now that the end was truly in sight, I could relax and enjoy myself for a change.

For the first time, I really felt as though the burden had been lifted from my shoulders, and I could look forward to peace and quiet.

We can all be deceived sometimes, however, into complacency and fail to realize that we are merely experiencing the lull before the storm.

I deserved to be able to enjoy life to its fullest, in light of the fact that I had certainly paid my dues on this project with the prospect of little, if any, financial gain. My reward was likely to be no more than the satisfaction of knowing that, in the face of enormous adversity, I had successfully executed a long-term project that had the potential to alter the course of boxing history.

Unfortunately, I had forgotten about protagonist Don King. As far I was concerned, this matter was now settled and no longer part of the picture, but King must have had his own ideas about the fight.

Contrary to what I expected, King was not out of the picture and indeed was maneuvering to be part of the action . . .

I had received a call from Charles Major, Jr. indicating that King had arrived in Freeport to meet with Berbick. I was furious! I left at 4:00 a.m. for the airport after saying goodbye to my wife. Because there were no planes to Freeport, we had to charter a flight. My trusted guard, who would have laid down his life for me if necessary, boarded the twin engine plane first. Our pilot, who was 21 years old, looked like a kid taking his first flight with a model airplane, but this "kid" flew us over the blue-green crystal clear waters of the Islands with the experience of a veteran flyer. When we landed at Freeport Airport, I thanked God and my pilot, in that order, and proceeded to Berbick's training, site, the Bahamas Princess Hotel. Charles had told me where Mr. King was staying. When I knocked on his door, Charles Lomax, the same Chicago attorney who had needled me from the start, answered. My guard escorted Mr. Lomax outside so I could chat with Mr. King who was on the telephone.

I had waited for a long time for this moment. Within a few seconds he finished his telephone conversation and, to my surprise, sprang from the bed and grabbed me by the collar, pressing me hard for $100,000.

Then everything went black. I could only remember blood running from his mouth like an open faucet which had apparently drenched my shirt.

I shouted, "I told you to leave us alone. We weren't bothering you. You have tried to wreck this promotion from day one."

Then I said in a calmer voice, "I am going to change my shirt and I will expect you to have your clothes packed by the time I return."

He looked at me in disgust and emphasized that I could not force him to go anywhere.

I said nothing and closed the door. I simply looked at Mr. Lomax with fire in my eyes.

I walked to Berbick's suite to change my shirt. Berbick cautiously thanked me for coming to Freeport. I returned to Mr. King's room and saw him ready and waiting at the front door. As we got on the elevator, I asked God for forgiveness and escorted King to a waiting taxi. I assured him and Mr. Lomax that they would be checked out of the hotel properly. The taxi driver had strict instructions to go to the Free-port Airport.

King's journey was recounted well in Dick Young's New York *Daily News* column on December 10. According to the sportswriter:

It happened in Freeport. Don King flew in there demanding a payoff and making threats. He had, he proclaimed, the legal power to stop the fight. He had, he claimed, a contract giving him promotional rights to Trevor Berbick's next fight, rights that stemmed from King's promotion of the Holmes-Berbick match last April.

Traditionally, when a promoter such as King or Bob Arum or, years ago, Mike Jacobs gives a challenger a crack at his fighter's title, said promoter always protects himself against the possibility of the title changing hands. This is done with an option clause in the contract, which stipulates that the promoter has the right to promote the boxer's next fights, or two or three fights. Sometimes the option right applies even should the crown not change hands.

It did not. Larry Holmes outpointed Berbick in 15 rounds at Las Vegas, winning about 13 of the rounds, but he had more trouble than expected with Berbick's awkward persistence.

When Ali picked Berbick as the opponent for his comeback, dollar signs flashed in Don King's eyes. "They're going to have to pay me some money if they want to put on that fight," he said, meaning the promoters, or Berbick, would be required to buy off King's option.

Thus it was that several days ago Don King came to the Bahamas to transact that little piece of business. He wound up in Freeport, Berbick's training site. He demanded, it is said, $200,000 as the buyout price.

THE ALTERNATIVE would be an injunction to stop the fight from taking place. Here, the details get a bit fuzzy. As best as can be reconstructed somebody made Don King an offer he couldn't refuse: Leave the Islands, pronto, in good health. King said he would not be intimidated.

Later that day, King had some visitors in his hotel room. They paid him off in a way he had not known since his youth in Cleveland, where one such punch-out resulted in a death that landed Don King in the slammer for seven years.

This time, Don King wound up, not in jail, but in a hospital. There are conflicting reports as to whether it took three, four or five men to persuade him to leave. Whatever, he flew out that night to Miami where he was given emergency treatment at the Broward Medical Center for head and facial wounds.

Berbick visiting with Youth & Sports Minister, the Honorable Senator Kendall W. Nottage. Photo supplied by Howard Bingham.

CHAPTER TEN

By Thursday our planned weigh-in was progressing on schedule. More than 400 members of the press gathered in the ballroom of the Britannia Beach. After most of the other fighters had weighted in, Berbick and Ali were ready. I walked over and hugged Berbick. It was an emotional moment.

Although Ali had accused Berbick of having "hen-house ways" the day before, he had nothing but favorable comments for his opponent at the weight-in. "I respect Berbick," Ali said. "I like him for giving me a chance."

"See, Berbick doesn't have much to say about me, or my religion. He's a nice guy who's always smiling. He's a real gentleman." Ali said, "I'll beat Berbick, I'll be dancin and dancin and jabbin all night."

Ali had said the day before that, "Berbick is slow—he can't beat me. I couldn't have picked a better opponent."

Today, however, a quiet calm-looking Ali said that all the talk was over. "This is a time for me to be real serious," he said. "All the talking and clowning around is over. I am very serious. I must be."

Ali cautiously stepped on the scales first. After Ali made his comments, it was Berbick's turn. One reporter wanted to know why Berbick had trained in Freeport. A reporter in the back whom I perceived as a troublemaker, wanted to know if Berbick had been paid. Berbick attempted to answer the question, but I interrupted by shouting, "Ask questions about the damn fight and not about the money!" As the room suddenly grew silent, Rahman whispered in my ear, "Damn James, be cool." I was relieved when the next question from the press dealt with a different subject. I took pleasure in having dispelled this troublesome matter. I ended the day with dinner.

Tomorrow was the big day for which I had fought, cried, lied and practically died for.

It was my last day as a fight promoter.

I started December 11 as I usually did every day, with prayer. I asked Almighty God to give me the strength to carry on not only through this day but through all the trial and tribulations that I faced in the days and years ahead.

I prayed for forgiveness for the many sins I had committed and for God's understanding of why I had failed him.

I asked the Almighty to overlook my shortcomings and to guide me and direct me to his ways. Had it not been for my faith in God and the support and understanding of my family, I would have never made it this far. I wanted the Father to know that I was truly thankful for all the many blessings he had bestowed upon me including good mental and physical health and a warm and loving wife and sons.

I had betrayed God so many times during the last several months, but I had always asked Him for forgiveness and I was prepared to accept the consequences of my acts.

While I had toiled and endured when everything seemed hopeless, God was due the credit for having made it possible for me to achieve this enormous task. "Please God," I prayed, "Stay by my side and show me the light. I am deeply indebted to you for all that you have done for me, and I now ask that you give me the power and the resolve to see this project through."

My Venture into fight promotion was coming to fruition, but I still had a few things to pull together. I dispatched Norman Thrasher to Miami to purchase the required boxing gloves and a ring bell.

Norman phoned in the early afternoon to tell me that following Mr. King's accident, Miami radio stations were reporting that Sports Internationale Bahamas, Limited had been locked out of the stadium and the fight would not take place. This was an obvious lie, but it was too late for me to do anything about it. I screamed, "Damn, I thought we had heard the last of Don King, I've sure got a lot to learn about the business of promoting."

Norman returned with the needed equipment and the fight was on. The story about the lock-out was typical of the media coverage the fight was getting in the United States. While the news stories in the Bahamian press were objective and generally positive, the information disseminated stateside was often harsh and unfair.

There was absolutely no factual basis for the story that the fight had been cancelled. In fact, if the reporters had bothered to check, they would have ascertained that the preparation and planning for the fight were going extremely well. We were right on schedule, and the Bahamian officials were bending over backwards to assist us in every way possible.

While I have generally held a healthy respect for the press in my country, including sportswriters, I lost most of that respect during this project. I know that it is often difficult for a reporter in the United States to thoroughly check a story that is developing in another country many miles away, but after all, there were tons of United States reporters right here in the Bahamas.

Were these journalists simply being lazy or was a "reliable source" misleading them? Any newsperson worth his or her salt should at least go to the original source—in this case, me—to get a confirmation or denial of the alleged facts. But, no one, of all the "responsible "journalists, ever contacted me or any of my assistants about this vicious rumor.

CHAPTER ELEVEN

Vivacious Jayne Kennedy visits the Champ and members of Sports Internationale, Bahamas Limited, the fight promoters. Photo supplied by Howard Bingham.

John Travolta, one of many celebrities present at Ali's last fight, visits with Ali and Cornelius. Photo supplied by Howard Bingham.

Ali and Cornelius aboard the yacht of renown world industrialist, anchored off Paradise Island, Assym Koshogi. Photo supplied by Howard Bingham.

Muhammad Ali, Ms. Jayne Kennedy, James Cornelius, and Cyril Ijeoma of Sports Internationale. Photo supplied by Howard Bingham.

I felt great now! I even selected a special suit for this glorious event. It was my big night, too.

The hotel was abuzz with excitement as the limos pulled up to take my family and other special guests to the Queen Elizabeth Sports Arena. As I closed the door to my suite, I heard what I thought was a gunshot coming from the Ali suite.

"Oh my God." I wondered, "Has anyone been shot?"

I hoped that some crazy individual had not breached the Champ's security and blown all we'd worked for.

I ran to Ali's suite and found that Howard Bingham, the person officially designated to dispense tickets for all Ali fights had been attacked by a crazy individual.

My mind reeled as I remembered that Ali fights were accompanied by chaos and bedlam caused by those individuals seeking tickets. The managers 'families needed special seats, the lawyers wanted seats, and, of course the Champ's family required special seating.

I was apprehensive, but all was well since the bullet had missed Howard and was lodged in a dresser. The gunman had been subdued by security guards.

I thought, "Wow, what a way to start a fight—with a BANG!"

Public figures such as Ali have to be closely guarded in this day and age when there are so many potential assassins. And even when security is tight, a determined individual can usually manage to get close enough to his target to pull off a shot.

When I heard the shot I recalled how easily such prominent individuals such as the Rev. Martin Luther King, Jr., President John F. Kennedy, Senator Robert Kennedy and Malcolm X had been murdered since 1960. Even President Kennedy's supposed assassin, Lee Harvey Oswald, was shot on live television, and more recently, Pope John Paul II and President Ronald

Reagan had been wounded.

Even though Howard escaped unscathed, the sound of the shot made me very nervous and uneasy. I already had butterflies in my stomach from worrying that something would go wrong at the last minute, and now my nerves were on edge.

With my adrenaline flowing and my heart thumping to high heaven, I felt like a walking zombie. There were dignitaries to greet and a huge crowd to face. It was unlikely I would ever have a chance to occupy the spotlight to the degree I would now.

I knew I could thrive in the bright lights and face the world since the fight was now a *fait accompli.*

As I reached the Queen Elizabeth Arena, I saw the joy on the face of the Sports Minister. I beamed with pride, not only for Ali and myself, but for the good I had brought to the Bahamas and its youth.

What a proud moment for the Caribbean!

I sauntered to the TV mobile unit, where I found Shelly Saltman.

"James, you finally got your show," he said.

During the fight my wife and I sat with the Police Commissioner and "Nine" Rolle, our invited guest.

I awaited anxiously my introduction from Mr. Carter of the Bahamian TV Network.

At last I heard him intone, "He traveled the world over, but the only place he could get an ear was here in Nassau. Ladies and Gentlemen, I bring you, the President of Sports Internationale Bahamas, Limited, the promoters of this event, Mr. James Cornelius."

It was a magic moment. I had come so far through so many difficulties. I savored the time but kept my comments brief since I was there to present a plaque to Mr. Nottage for his courage in issuing the license for the fight. I strolled to Ali's corner, for the last time. All the while I prayed that God would protect my hero and that both of us would taste the sweetness of victory again.

For ten rounds Muhammad Ali battled the awkward bruiser.

You could hear people at ringside rejoicing over the size of Ali's heart.

In round one Ali threw more punches than he did in the entire fight with Larry Holmes.

I had proven my point October 10, 1980.

Ali was sick; something was wrong.

I did not even attend the press conference the next morning.

There was no need.

I had seen my hero fight a gallant battle, only to lose with unbearable pain. The critics had been right in their predictions of Ali's defeat, and the night and subsequent days were sheer sadness for me. The great gladiator had been humiliated for now but America could be proud that he had attempted the impossible. Although he failed in the end, the Champ would remain a genuine hero in the eyes of those who loved him, including myself. In many ways, his fate had already been sealed but all of us had failed to heed the warning signals.

The one and only Muhammad Ali was a victim of a brutal and destructive sport that has consumed many, men. He remains, however, a symbol of hope and humanity for all Americans, not just black Americans. Muhammad Ali is more than a reflection of the American spirit.

He *is* the American spirit that lives in us all.

THE END

Dedication

This book is dedicated to Muhammad Ali, one of the greatest athletes known to mankind, and whose superior athletic abilities are unmatched. But Ali is more than an athlete. He has successfully championed many moral causes that demonstrate his humaneness and his humanness.

My sincere thanks to the people of the Bahamas and especially the people in Nassau for all of their prayers, confidence and hard work which made "The Last Punch" dream a reality. I also dedicate this work to my many friends, who throughout the years have always lent a helping hand.

A special commendation to my wife for the many hours of labor put into this project, her support over the years and her understanding while I experienced many changes.

Finally, a special dedication to a dear and anonymous friend, without whose encouragement, assistance, and general counseling this book could not have been completed.

In memory of

Trevor Berbick (August 1, 1954 – October 28, 2006) was a Jamaican-Canadian heavyweight boxer.

William Everett Bannister

William "Life" Curtiss

Charles Major Sr.

Donald "Nine" Rolle

Levoine "Bowe" Stuart